John F. Dillon

Removal of Causes from State Courts to Federal Courts

with forms adapted to the several acts of Congress on the subject. Second

Edition

John F. Dillon

Removal of Causes from State Courts to Federal Courts
with forms adapted to the several acts of Congress on the subject. Second Edition

ISBN/EAN: 9783337234515

Printed in Europe, USA, Canada, Australia, Japan

Cover: Foto ©Suzi / pixelio.de

More available books at **www.hansebooks.com**

FROM

STATE COURTS TO FEDERAL COURTS,

*With Forms Adapted to the Several Acts of
Congress on the Subject.*

SECOND AND REVISED EDITION.

BY JOHN F. DILLON,

CIRCUIT JUDGE OF THE EIGHTH JUDICIAL CIRCUIT, AUTHOR OF A TREATISE
ON "MUNICIPAL CORPORATIONS," ETC.

ST. LOUIS:
THE CENTRAL LAW JOURNAL.
1877.

PUBLISHER'S PREFATORY NOTE.

The editor of the SOUTHERN LAW REVIEW requested the author to prepare, for that magazine, a practical paper on the Removal of Causes from State Courts to Federal Courts, under the principal statutes of Congress on that subject. The article was accordingly written, and appeared in the SOUTHERN LAW REVIEW for July, 1876. An extra edition of several hundred copies was separately struck off, and was speedily exhausted. At the request of the present publisher, the author of the Tract has revised and enlarged it, bringing into view more fully the State Court decisions, adding the decisions of the Federal Courts down to date, a Table of Cases and of Contents, an Index and an Appendix of Forms. This will make it more convenient and useful to the profession, for whose benefit it was originally written, and is now republished.

CONTENTS.

TABLE OF CASES CITED.

REMOVAL OF SUITS

From State Courts to Federal Courts.

SECTION I.

THE FEDERAL JUDICIAL SYSTEM—ITS GROWTH AND IMPORTANCE.

The Act of September 24, 1789 (1 Stats. at Large, 79), styled by way of eminence the Judiciary Act, was passed the same year in which the Constitution went into effect, and organized the National or Federal Judicial System, substantially as it exists to-day. No structural changes have since been made in that system, and considering the complex and highly artificial nature of the Federal jurisdiction, the Judiciary Act is justly to be regarded as one of the most remarkable instances of wise, sagacious, thoroughly considered legislative enactments in the history of the law. But while the National Judicial System as established by that act remains without organic changes, yet changes of a minor, though important character have been made from time to time. This has been done, however, without disturbing the nice adjustments and skillful arrangements of the original plan. The system of 1789 is, in form and essence, the system of 1876. If we consider the intricate nature of the relations of the Federal and State governments; that each has a judicial system of its own; that the two classes of courts sit in the same territory, and exercise day by day jurisdiction over the same subjects and the same persons; that the judicial system provided by the Judiciary Act was untried and experimental; that serious conflicts between the State and Federal courts have been almost wholly avoided; that the Judiciary Act remains, after the lapse of nearly a century, almost intact,—it will appear that the admiration with which it has been regarded by statesmen, lawyers and judges, is not undeserved. And the changes which have been made are those which have been demanded by convenience, by the increase of the population and business of the country, and, during and since the War of the Rebellion, by circumstances brought about by that unanticipated event, and they are not changes made necessary by want of foresight in the great minds which devised and enacted the original scheme. The altered condition of the country has made still further changes, or rather *enlargements*, of the plan necessary, such as, for example, an intermediate court of appeals, for the relief of the Supreme Court and the convenience of suitors, and more judicial force in the districts, etc.; but it is not the purpose of this paper to enter upon this topic.

The amendments to the Judiciary Act made from time to time by Congress concerning the Federal courts, and notably those made during and since the Rebellion, have tended uniformly in one direction, namely, an enlargement of their jurisdiction. And the recent act of March 3, 1875, in connection with the legislation then existing, has amplified the Federal judicial power almost to the full limits of the constitution. The history of the Federal jurisdiction is one of constant growth: slow, indeed, during the first half-century and more, but very rapid within the last few years. For various reasons, which we need not stop to indicate, the small tide of litigation that formerly flowed in Federal channels has swollen into a mighty stream. Certain it is that of late years the importance of the Federal courts has rapidly increased, and that much, perhaps most, of the great litigations of the country is now conducted in them. This is noticeably so in the Western states. These observations have been made, because they are a fitting introduction to the special topic we have placed at the head of this article,— *Removal of Causes from the State Courts.* They have, indeed, been suggested by that topic ; for, as will be seen as we proceed, the limited right in this regard given by the Judiciary Act has been enlarged from time to time, until a very considerable portion of the contested cases in the Federal courts now reach them through this channel.

The editor of the SOUTHERN LAW REVIEW, in consequence of the recent changes in the legislation on this important subject, and the uncertainty which many lawyers suppose to surround it in consequence of those changes, has requested the writer to prepare a practical article which shall exhibit the present state of the law concerning the *Right* to removal and the *Mode* of making that right available.

The cognizance over cases removed to the Federal court has sometimes been referred to the *appellate* jurisdiction, on the ground that, as the suit is not instituted in the Federal court by original process, the jurisdiction of that court must be appellate ;[1] but Mr. Justice Nelson accurately characterized the jurisdiction in such cases " original jurisdiction, acquired indirectly by a removal from the State court."[2]

SECTION II.

THE PRINCIPAL STATUTES ON THE SUBJECT OF REMOVALS—ACTS OF 1789, 1866, 1867 AND 1875.

There are some statutes giving the right of removal in special cases which we shall only mention generally, such as the right to remove causes, civil and criminal, in any State court, against persons denied *Civil Rights;*[3] and suits, civil

---

[1] Martin v. Hunter's Lessee, 1 Wheat. 304, 349, 350.

[2] Dennistoun v. Draper, 5 Blatchf. 336; Fisk v. U. P. R. R. Co., 6 Blatchf. 362, 367.

[3] U. S. Rev. Stats., secs. 641, 642, construed. State v. Gaines, 2 Woods C. C. 342, (1874) ; Gaughan v. N. W. Fertilizing Co., 3 Bissell, 485, (1873) ; Fowlkes v. Fowlkes, 8 Chicago Legal News, 41; Commonwealth v. Artman, 3 Grant (Pa.), 436; Hodgson v. Milward, 3 Grant (Pa.), 418.

and criminal, against *Revenue Officers* of the United States, and against officers and other persons acting under the *Registration Laws;*[4] and suits by *Aliens* against *Civil Officers* of

[4] Rev. Stats., title XXVI, "The Elective Franchise." Rev. Stats., sec. 643.

Act of March 2, 1833 (4 Stats. at Large, 633), known as the "*force act.*" This act provided for the removal of suits and prosecutions commenced in a court of any state, against any officer of the United States, for any act done under the *revenue* laws of the United States, or under color thereof. See. Rev. Stats., sec. 643. This statute, as re-enacted, applies to the removal of *revenue cases* under "*any* revenue law of the United States." Rev. Stats.. sec. 643. It was previously held to be in force as to removal of revenue cases, except those arising under the internal revenue system. Peyton v. Bliss, 1 Woolw. 170 (1868), Miller, J.; Stevens v. Mack. 5 Blatchf. 514 (1867), Benedict, J.

Construction of act of 1833. see Dennistoun v. Draper, 5 Blatchf. 336, Nelson, J.; Abranches v. Schell, 4 Blatchf. 256; Wood v. Matthews. 2 Blatchf. 370. The removal may be had without regard to the *amount* in controversy. Wood v. Matthews, 2 Blatchf. 370.

A suit against an officer of the United States is not removable under the act of 1833 on the ground that the act complained of was done under the *instructions of the treasury department.* Victor v. Cisco, 5 Blatchf. 128—but see Rev. Stats., sec. 643. See Benchley v. Gilbert (Act of July 13, 1866, sec. 67), 8 Blatchf. 147; Salt Co. v. Wilkinson, 8 Blatchf. 30.

· Cases arising under *direct tax* law are removable under act of 1833. Peyton v. Bliss, 1 Woolw. 170. Miller, J.

What are "*revenue laws*" under the act of March 2, 1833? That Act extends to an action in the State court against a postmaster for a wrongful refusal to deliver a letter to the plaintiff, and such an action was held to be removable into the Federal court. Warner v. Fowler, 4 Blatchf. 311 (1859). Ingersoll, J.

An *action of slander* begun in a State court against a *collector of customs.* for words spoken while in the discharge of his official duty and explanatory of it. may be transferred to the Federal court under the "force act" of March 2. 1833 (4 Stats. at Large, 633), which provides, "that any case where suit or prosecution shall be commenced in a court of any state against any officer of the United States, for or on account of any act done under the revenue laws of the United States, or under color thereof." may be removed by the defendant to the Federal court. The question arose on a motion to remand; and as it appeared from the petition for the removal that the words complained of were spoken by the defendant. while in the discharge of his official duties as collector. and in connection with a seizure of goods for an alleged violation of the revenue laws (which fact the motion to remand necessarily admitted to be true). the court held that words thus spoken were to be

the United States under specified circumstances ;⁵ and suits against certain *Federal Corporations*, or their members as such members, may be removed upon verified petition, " stating that such defendant has a defense arising under or by virtue of the Constitution or of any treaty or law of the United States."⁶

This act is not repealed by the act of March 3, 1875.⁷

It applies, in its true construction, only to corporations considered, under the statute, *as an act done under the revenue laws* of the United States. Woods, Circuit Judge, says: " Words spoken in connection with the act of seizure, and in explanation or justification thereof, become part of the act, and together with the seizure form one transaction." Buttner v. Miller, 1 Woods C. C. 620 (1871).

Act of March 3, 1863 (12 Stats. at Large, 757), and act of March 2, 1867, as to removability of suits for acts done *during the late rebellion* under Federal authority. See Milligan v. Hovey, 3 Bissell, 13; s. c., 3 Ch. Legal News, 321; Clark v. Dick (limitation), 1 Dill. C. C. 8; Woodson v. Fleet, 2 Abb. U. S. 15; Bigelow v. Forrest (ejectment suit not removable), 9 Wall. 339 (1869); Murray v. Patrie (removal after judgment), 5 Blatchf. 343 (1866), reversed in The Justices v. Murray, 9 Wall. 274 (1869). This last case holds that so much of the 5th section of the Act of March 3 (1863), as provides for the removal of a *judgment* in a State court, where the cause was tried by a jury, for re-trial on the facts and law in the Circuit court, is in conflict with the seventh amendment of the Constitution, and void. McKee v. Rains, 10 Wall. 22; Galpin v. Critchlow, 112 Mass. 341 (1873); Wetherbee v. Johnson, 14 Mass. 412; The Mayor v. Cooper, 6 Wall. 247; Lamar v. Dana, 10 Blatchf. 34; Bell v. Dix, 49 N. Y. 232; Anthon v. Morton, 15 Am. Law Reg. (N. S.), 556; Hodgson v. Milward, 3 Grant (Pa.), 418. Criminal case can not be removed before indictment found in the State court. Commonwealth v. Artman, 3 Grant (Pa,), 436.

⁵ Rev. Stats., sec. 644.

⁶ Act of July 27, 1868. (15 Stats. at Large, 227; Rev. Stats., sec. 640.) This statute, as found in sec. 640 of the Revised Statutes, is as follows: "Any suit commenced in any court other than a Circuit or District court of the United States against any corporation other than a banking corporation, organized under a law of the United States, or against any member thereof as such member, for any alleged liability of such corporation, or of such member as a member thereof, may be removed, for trial, in the Circuit court for the district where such suit is pending, upon the petition of such defendant, verified by oath, stating that such defendant has a defense arising under or by virtue of the Constitution or of any treaty or law of the United States. Such removal, in all other respects, shall be governed by the provisions of the preceding section."

⁷ Kain v. Texas Pacific R. R. Co., 3 Cent. L. J. 12, Duval, J.

organized under a law of Congress, and does not include national banks, which are expressly excepted, nor corporations created by foreign governments or by the several states.[8]

Under this act Mr. Justice Nelson decided at the circuit two important points, which we notice, as they illustrate more or less questions which arise under other removal acts, and particularly the act of March 3, 1875. He held : 1st. Where one or more of the defendants have presented a petition for removal conforming to the act, and thus initiated the removal, it is not competent for the State court to take any proceedings in the cause, other than to perfect the removal, as the other defendants may appear and present their petitions, which they may do at different times.   2d. That the joining of defendants in a suit, not within the limitations of the act, with those who are, can not have the effect to defeat the Federal jurisdiction. He adds : " If this were permitted, the privilege extended to parties setting up a right under the Constitution and Laws of the United States, would, in most, if not in every instance, be defeated," and " most of these removal acts, depending principally upon the *subject-matter*, and intended to secure the interpretation of the Constitution and Laws of the United States, at the original hearing, to its own judiciary, would be futile and worthless." In such cases, " if these outside parties are deemed material, or are really material, to a complete remedy in behalf of the plaintiff, they must be regarded as subordinate and incidental to the principal litigation in respect to which the act of Congress has interposed the remedy of removal.   In this way the right of the parties to have their defense, under the Constitution or Laws of the United States, tried in the Federal courts, is secured : and, at the same time, the remedy of the plaintiff is unimpaired.'"[9]

---

[8] Jones v. Oceanic Steam Nav. Co.. 11 Blatchf. 406 (1873).

[9] Fisk v. Union Pacific R. R. Co.. 8 Blatchf. 243, 248 (1871). The act of July 27, 1868 (Rev. Stats. 640). held to provide only for a case in which the federal corporation or member thereof was the *sole defendant*.   Haz-

A petition for removal under this act must state that the corporation or member thereof applying for removal has "a defense arising under or by virtue of the Constitution of the United States or some treaty or law of the United States;" but it need not state what the defense is, nor the facts constituting it :—this is a matter for determination in the Federal court, not on motion to remand, but on formal pleadings, or pleadings and proof.[10]

The important acts of general operation as to removals, and which relate to cases that daily arise, are what is known as the 12th section of the Judiciary Act : the act of July 27,

ard v. Durant *et al.*. 9 R. 1. 602. 609 (1868). by Potter, J. But it was decided otherwise in Fisk v. Union Pacific Railroad Co., 6 Blatchf. 362; s. c. 8 *ib*. 243. 299; and this latter is, undoubtedly, the true construction of the act on this point.

[10] Jones v. Oceanic Steam Nav. Co.. 11 Blatchf. 406. See on this point The Mayor v. Cooper, 6 Wall. 247: Dennistoun v. Draper. 5 Blatchf. 336, Nelson, J.; Turton v. Union Pacific R. R. Co.. 3 Dillon. C. C. 366, Miller. J. Compare Magee v. U. P. R. R. Co.. 2 Sawyer. 447. Hillyer, J.; Hazard v. Durant *et al.*, 9 R. I. 602, before Potter, J.; Kain v. Texas Pacific R. R. Co. (East. Dist. Texas. Duval. J.). 3 Cent. L. J. 12 (1875); Fisk v. U. P. R. R. Co.. 8 Blatchf. 243: *Ib*. 299. Under this act, Hillyer, J., decided that the fact, that the corporation (the Union Pacific Railroad Co.) was one organized under a law of the United States. is not enough to authorize the transfer of a cause to the Circuit court of the United States. The action was one for a personal injury to the plaintiff; and it appearing that the only defense made by the answer was in denial of the imputed negligence. the decision of which depended entirely upon common-law principles. and not upon the construction of any act of Congress. the cause was. on motion, remanded to the State court. Magee v. U. P. R. R. Co.. 2 Sawyer, C. C. 447 (1873). Under the same state of facts. Mr. Justice Miller has held precisely the other way. Turton v. U. P. R. R. Co.. 3 Dillon. C. C. 366 (1875). The question is a close one: and the suggestion presents itself, if in every suit against a federal corporation, such a corporation necessarily has a defense under a law of the United States. because it is a corporation organized under a law of the United States. why did Congress not unconditionally provide for the transfer of all suits. without requiring a verified statement that they have "a defense arising under or by virtue of the Constitution or a treaty or a law of the United States?" As bearing on this subject. see Osborn v. U. S. Bank, 9 Wheat. 738; Cohens v. Virginia. 6 Wheat. 264: Hazard v. Durant *et al.*. 9 R. 1. 602; Kain v. Texas Pacific R. R. Co., 3 Cent. L. J. 12 (1875) ; Fisk v. Union Pacific R. R. Co., 6 Blatchf. 362; s. c. 8 *id*. 243. 299. The view

1866,[11] the act of March 2, 1867,[12] known as the "prejudice or local influence act," and lastly the act of March 3, 1875.[13] This last named act was passed since the Revised Statutes, and consequently is not to be found therein. The 12th section of the Judiciary Act, the act of July 27, 1866, and of March 2, 1867, above mentioned, although technically repealed by the Revised Statutes of the United States, are substantially re-enacted in the 639th section thereof. These statutes are the foundation of the law on the subject of removals on the grounds therein provided for, and the principal purpose of this article is to give a *reading* on those statutes, or, in other words, an exposition of their meaning in the light of the adjudications which have been made under them.

The text of these statutes is so essential to an understanding of the subject, that we reproduce, for convenience, the more material portions of them in a note.[14]

of Mr. Justice Miller in the case of Turton, *supra*, derives strong support in the consideration that, under its charter, this corporation may sue and be sued originally in the Circuit court, without reference to citizenship or other ground of jurisdiction (Bauman v. Union Pacific R. R. Co., 3 Dillon, 367), and jurisdiction by removal is but the exercise of original jurisdiction acquired in this manner. *Ante*, sec. 1.

[11] 14 Stats. at Large, 306.

[12] 14 Stats. at Large, 558.

[13] Acts of 1875, p. 470.

[14] Section 639 of the Revised Statutes is as follows: "Any suit commenced in any State court, wherein the amount in dispute, exclusive of costs, exceeds the sum or value of five hundred dollars, to be made to appear to the satisfaction of said court, may be removed for trial into the Circuit court for the district where such suit is pending, next to be held after the filing of the petition for such removal hereinafter mentioned, in the cases and in the manner stated in this section.

"*First.* When the suit is against an alien or is by a citizen of the state wherein it is brought, and against a citizen of another state, it may be removed on the petition of such defendant, filed in said state court at the time of entering his appearance in said State court." [This is, substantially, section 12 of the Judiciary Act.]

"*Second.* When the suit is against an alien and a citizen of the state wherein it is brought, or is by a citizen of such state against a citizen of the same, and a citizen of another state, it may be so removed, as against said alien or citizen of another state, upon the petition of such defend-

SECTION III.

VALIDITY OF THE REMOVAL ACTS—RIGHTS PROTECTED FROM INVASION OR DENIAL BY THE STATES.

The power of Congress to authorize the transfer of cases, to which the Federal judicial power conferred by the Constitution extends, from the State courts to the Federal courts, has been frequently declared by the Supreme Court, and the constitutionality of the removal acts of 1789, 1833, 1863,

ant, filed at any time before the trial or final hearing of the cause, if, so far as it relates to him, it is brought for the purpose of restraining or enjoining him, or is a suit in which there can be a final determination of the controversy so far as concerns him, without the presence of the other defendants as parties in the cause. But such removal shall not take away or prejudice the right of the plaintiff to proceed at the same time with the suit in the State court, as against the other defendants." [This is, substantially, the act of July 27, 1866.]

" *Third.* When a suit is between a citizen of the state in which it is brought, and a citizen of another state, it may be so removed on the petition of the latter, whether he be plaintiff or defendant, filed at any time before the trial or final hearing of the suit, if before or at the time of filing said petition he makes and files in said State court an affidavit stating that he has reason to believe, and does believe that, from prejudice or local influence, he will not be able to obtain justice in such State court." [This is, substantially, the act of March 2, 1867.]

Section 639 of the Revised Statutes continues as follows: " In order to such removal, the petitioner in the cases aforesaid must, at the time of filing his petition therefor, offer in said State court good and sufficient surety for his entering in such Circuit court, on the first day of its session, copies of said process against him, and of all pleadings, depositions, testimony and other proceedings in the cause, or, in said cases where a citizen of the state in which the suit is brought is a defendant, copies of all process, pleadings, depositions, testimony, and other proceedings in the cause concerning or affecting the petitioner, and also for his there appearing and entering special bail in the cause, if special bail was originally requisite therein. It shall thereupon be the duty of the State court to accept the surety and to proceed no further in the cause against the petitioner, and any bail that may have been originally taken shall be discharged. When the said copies are entered as aforesaid in the Circuit court, the cause shall there proceed in the same manner as if it had been brought there by original process, and the copies of pleadings shall have the same force and effect, in every respect and for every purpose, as the original pleadings would have had by the laws and practice of the courts of such state if the cause had remained in the State court."

1866 and 1867, is established beyond question. "The validity of this legislation," says Mr. Justice Field, "is not open to serious question, and the provisions adopted have been recognized and followed, with scarcely an exception, by the Federal and State courts since the establishment of the government.' [15]

Act of March 3, 1875. The second and third sections of this act in relation to the removal of actions are as follows: "§ 2. That any suit of a civil nature, at law or in equity, now pending or hereafter brought in any State court, where the matter in dispute exceeds, exclusive of costs, the sum or value of five hundred dollars, and arising under the Constitution or laws of the United States, or treaties made, or which shall be made, under their authority, or in which the United States shall be plaintiff or petitioner, or in which there shall be a controversy between citizens of different states, or a controversy between citizens of the same state claiming lands under grants of different states, or a controversy between citizens of a state and foreign states, citizens or subjects, either party may remove said suit into the Circuit court of the United States for the proper district; and when in any suit mentioned in this section there shall be a controversy which is wholly between citizens of different states, and which can be fully determined as between them, then either one or more of the plaintiffs or defendants, actually interested in such controversy, may remove said suit to the Circuit court of the United States for the proper district."

"§ 3. *Removal—Proceedings.*—That whenever either party, or any one or more of the plaintiffs or defendants entitled to remove any suits mentioned in the next preceding section, shall desire to remove such suit from a State court to the Circuit court of the United States, he or they may make or file a petition in such suit in such State court before or at the term at which said cause could be first tried and before the trial thereof, for the removal of such suit into the Circuit court to be held in the district where such suit is pending, and shall make and file therewith a bond, with good and sufficient surety, for his or their entering in such Circuit court, on the first day of its then next session, a copy of the record in such suit, and for paying all costs that may be awarded by the said Circuit court, if said court shall hold that such suit was wrongfully or improperly removed thereto, and also for there appearing and entering special bail in such suit, if special bail was originally requisite therein. It shall then be the duty of the State court to accept said petition and bond, and proceed no further in such suit, and any bail that may have been originally taken shall be discharged; and the said copy being entered as aforesaid in said Circuit court of the United States, the cause shall then proceed in the same manner as if it had been originally commenced in the said Circuit court," etc., etc.

[15] Gaines v. Fuentes *et al.*, U. S. Sup. Court, Oct. Term, 1875, 3 Cent. L. J. 371; s. c. 2 Otto, 10. See also Sewing Machine Companies' Case, 18 Wall.

In this connection, it may also be observed that the right to remove cases into the Federal court, when the terms upon which the right is given by the acts of Congress in that behalf are complied with, can not be defeated by state legislation. Therefore, a State statute which allows an insurance company to do business in the state only on condition that it will agree not to remove suits against it to the Federal courts, is unconstitutional, and such an agreement, though entered into by the company, is void.[16]

SECTION IV.

MATERIAL ELEMENTS OF THE RIGHT, AS GIVEN BY THE PRINCIPAL STATUTES.

The material elements of the statutes on this subject, it will be perceived, are the *nature of the suits* which may be removed ; the *amount* or *value* in dispute ; the *parties* to the suit, and in this connection the *party entitled* to the removal ; the *time* when the application must be made ; the *mode* of making the application, and herein of the *surety* or *bond*, etc., required, and the *effect on the jurisdiction* of the State court and of the Federal court of a proper application to remove a cause which is removable.

553; Johnson v. Monell. 1 Woolw. 394; Meadow Valley Co. v. Dodds. 7 Nev. 143; Chicago etc. Railway Co. v. Whitton's Admr.. 13 Wall. 270; The Mayor v. Cooper. 6 Wall. 247.

[16] Insurance Co. v. Morse, 20 Wall. 445. See also Insurance Co. v. Dunn. 19 Wall. 214; Gordon v. Longest. 16 Pet. 97; Kanouse v. Martin. 14 How. 23; s. c., 15 How. 198; Stevens v. Phoenix Insurance Co.. 41 N. Y. 149; Holden v. Putnam Insurance Co.. 46 N. Y. 1; Hadley v. Dunlap. 10 Ohio St. 1. Home Insurance Co. v. Davis. 29 Mich. 238. is inconsistent with Insurance Co. v. Morse, *supra*. In Hartford Fire Ins. Co. v. Doyle (West. Dist. Wis.. Hopkins. J.). 3 Cent. L. J. 41. an act of the legislature of the state. making it the duty of the secretary of state to revoke licenses of companies for removing suits to Federal courts. was held void. and such revocation restrained by injunction.

SECTION V.

THE 12TH SECTION OF THE JUDICIARY ACT.

Before entering in detail upon the several elements of the removal enactments, it is advisable to advert to some general considerations touching these several statutes. We commence with section 12 of the Judiciary Act. The reader may recur to its language as re-enacted in substance in the Revised Statutes, given in a note to a preceding section; and it is important to remember that from 1789 until the act of July 27, 1866, above mentioned, the 12th section of the Judiciary Act was the only statute authorizing the removal of causes from the State courts to the Circuit court of the United States, on the ground of *citizenship* of the parties.

Section 12 of the Judiciary Act, omitting the case of aliens, authorized the removal by the *defendant* (under limitations therein mentioned), where the suit is commenced in the State court *" by a citizen of the state in which the suit is brought, against a citizen of another state."* That is, if the suit is by a resident plaintiff, the *non-resident* defendant may have it removed; but the resident plaintiff could not. Under section 11 of the Judiciary Act as to *original* suits in the Circuit court, a *non-resident* plaintiff might sue in the Circuit court a *resident defendant;* but if the non-resident plaintiff elected to sue in a State court, section 12 of that act gave *neither* party the right to remove the cause from the State court to a court of the United States. The plaintiff was not given the right, because he had voluntarily selected the State court in which to bring his action; the defendant was not given the right, because it was not supposed that *he* would have any grounds to object that he was sued in the courts of his own state. So that the right of removal by the 12th section of the Judiciary Act is limited to the non-resident citizen when sued by a resident plaintiff in the courts of the state. By section 11 of the Judiciary Act, the Circuit court.

has jurisdiction when the suit is between a citizen of the state in which it is brought and a citizen of another state. This was construed by the courts to mean that, if there were several plaintiffs and several defendants, *each one of each class* must possess the requisite character as to citizenship.[17] For example, a citizen of New York and a citizen of Georgia could not join as plaintiffs in suing in New York a citizen of Massachusetts, if found in New York, because the plaintiffs were not each competent to sue; for the citizen of Georgia could not, under section 11 of the Judiciary Act, sue a citizen of Massachusetts in New York.[18] Some of the more important cases touching the jurisdiction of the Circuit court under the 11th section of the Judiciary Act, and concerning the effect of the act of 1839 (5 Stats. at Large, 321), which relates to suits commenced in the Circuit court, are referred to in the note, as they have a bearing on the construction of the 12th section.[19]

[17] Strawbridge v. Curtiss. 3 Cranch. 267; Coal Co. v. Blatchford. 11 Wall. 172.

[18] Moffat v. Soley, 2 Paine, C. C. 103. This restriction on the jurisdiction of the Federal courts is removed by the act of March 3, 1875, and now these courts would have jurisdiction of such a suit as that mentioned in the text.

[19] The case of the Commercial Bank v. Slocomb, 14 Pet. 60 (except so far as it has been since overruled as to the suability of corporations in the Federal courts), holds, and only holds, that under the Judiciary Act the jurisdiction of the Circuit court is defeated if some of the defendants are citizens of the *same state with the plaintiff*; and that this principle was not changed by the act of February 28, 1839. Same principle affirmed, at the same term, in a case rightly decided. Irvine v. Lowry, 14 Pet. 293. See, also, Clearwater v. Meredith, 21 How. 489. In Taylor v. Cook *et al.*, 2 McLean, 516, the plaintiffs were citizens of *New York*, and brought suit in the Circuit court of the United States in *Illinois* against Cook, a citizen of *Illinois*, and Spaulding, a citizen of *Missouri*, who entered a voluntary appearance, and the question was, whether the court had jurisdiction, and, aided by the act of 1839, it was held that it had. Judge McLean, in delivering his opinion says, *arguendo*, that prior to the act of 1839, and under the 11th section of the Judiciary Act limiting the jurisdiction to suits between " a citizen of the state where the suit is brought and a citizen of another state," as construed, " the court could not take jurisdiction of the case; for as between the plaintiffs who are citizens of New York, and the defendant, Spaulding, who is a citizen of Missouri.

But it should be borne in mind that in cases remo ed from the State courts the *jurisdiction of the Circuit court is dependent upon the act under which the suit is removed*, and not upon the legislation which confers jurisdiction upon that court in cases originally brought therein ; and therefore the restrictions on the jurisdiction in the 11th section of the Judiciary Act have no application to cases removed under the 12th section of that act.[20]

Under section 12 of the Judiciary Act regulating removals, it is settled that a cause can not be removed thereunder unless *all* the defendants ask for it ; that to bring the case within the act *all* the plaintiffs must be citizens of the state in which suit is brought, and *all* of the defendants must be *citizens* of some other *state* or *states*.[21] But this rule, we may remark in passing, does not apply to persons who are mere nominal or formal parties.[22]

the court could exercise no jurisdiction in the state of Illinois; because in that case neither party would reside in the state where suit is brought." But see *contra*, the observations, *arguendo*, of Wayne, J., in Louisville Railroad Company v. Letson, 2 Howard, on pp. 553, 554, in which he concludes that it is not necessary under the Judiciary Act that all of the defendants should be citizens of the same state, provided none of them are citizens of the same state with the plaintiff. (See *infra*, sec. 8.) The joinder of a defendant not served, and who does not appear, who is a citizen of the *same state* with the plaintiff, does not defeat the jurisdiction of the Circuit court; at all events, it does not since the act of 1839, Doremus v. Bennett, 4 McLean, 224. But the joinder of *such* a defendant who is served, if he be not a mere nominal defendant, does defeat the jurisdiction; at all events, it did prior to the act of March 3, 1875, Ketchum v. Farmers' etc. Co., 4 McLean, 1: Coal Co. v. Blatchford, 11 Wall. 172: Sewing Machine Co. Case, 18 Wall. 553.

[20] Green v. Custard, 23 How. 484: Barclay v. Levee Commissioners, 1 Woods C. C. 254: Bushnell v. Kennedy, 9 Wall. 387; Sands v. Smith, 1 Dillon, 293, 297: Sayles v. N. W. Ins. Co. 2 Curtis. C. C. 212; Gaines v. Fuentes, U. S. Sup. Court, Oct. term, 1875, 2 Otto, 10, 3 Cent. L. J. 271: Winans v. McKean, etc., Nav. Co. 6 Blatchf. 215.

[21] Beardsley v. Torrey, 4 Wash. 286, (1822): Ward v. Arredondo, 1 Paine, 410 (1825): Hubbard v. R. R. Co., 3 Blatchf. 84; s. c. 25 Vt. 715, (1853): Beery v. Irick, 22 Gratt. 484: *Ex parte* Girard. 3 Wall. Jr. 263; Smith v. Rines, 2 Summ. 330: Hazard v. Durant. 9 R. I. 602; *In re* Turner, 3 Wall. Jr. 260; *Ib.* 263.

[22] Browne v. Strode, 5 Cranch, 303: Wormley v. Wormley, 8 Wheat. 421: Ward v. Arredondo, *supra* ; Wood v. Davis, 18 How. 467. *Who are*

Omitting the case of aliens, it will be perceived that the 12th section of the Judiciary Act (now Rev. Stat., Sec. 639, sub-division 1), gave the power of removal only under the following circumstances:

1. The plaintiffs, or if more than one, then all of the plaintiffs must be citizens of the state in which the suit is brought;

2. The defendants, or if more than one, then *all* of the defendants must be citizens of another state or states;

3. It is limited to *civil* suits, involving, besides costs, a sum or value exceeding $500;

4. The right of removal is limited to the *defendant* or de-

nominal parties and who are not, see also Bixby v. Couse, 8 Blatchf. 73; Coal Co. v. Blatchford, 11 Wall. 172; Davis v. Gray, 16 Wall. 220; Weed Sewing Machine Co. v. Wicks, 3 Dillon. 261, 266; Knapp v. Troy & Boston R. R. Co., Sup. Court, Oct. Term, 1873, 20 Wall. 117; where the cases are cited by Mr. Justice Davis. In this last case, the learned judge speaking of the removal act of 1867, says, " it does not change the settled rule that determines who are to be regarded as the plaintiff and the defendant; and as the plaintiff and defendant in this action were both citizens of New York, the Circuit court had no jurisdiction to entertain it." 20 Wall. 124. The fact that defendants are named who have not been served, or have not appeared, and who are citizens of the same state with the plaintiff, will not defeat the right of removal. *Ex parte* Girard, 3 Wall. Jr. 263 (1858). Grier, J.

Nominal parties, or persons made parties who are not necessary to a determination of the real controversy, will not defeat the right to a removal. Mayor etc. v. Cummins, 47 Ga. 321 (1872); Wood v. Davis, 18 How. 467 (1855); Ward v. Arredondo, 1 Paine, 410 (1825), Mr. Justice Thompson.

Fraudulent or improper joinder of parties to prevent removal. See Smith v. Rines, 2 Sumner, 338; *Ex parte* Girard, 3 Wall. Jr. 263. *Improper joinder of causes of action.* Cooke v. State Nat. Bank, 52 N. Y. 96 (1873).

Officers of a corporation, joined with it as defendants to a bill in equity, but as to whom no relief was prayed in their individual capacity, and no relief which was not asked as against the corporation, are nominal parties in such a sense, as not to defeat the right of removal, if the right otherwise exists. Hatch v. Ch., R. I. & P. R. R. Co., 6 Blatchf. 105 (1868).

As to effect, under the act of July 27, 1868, as to removal of cases by *Federal corporations*, or the joinder of defendants who do not possess the right of removal, see *ante*, sec. 2, and note.

2

fendants, and must be exercised or applied for by *all* of the defendants.[23]

5. The petition for the removal must be filed *at the time* the defendant or defendants *enter their appearance* in the State court.[24] Hence, if some of the plaintiffs were not citizens of the state in which the suit was brought; or if some of the defendants were citizens of the same state with plain-

[23] Smith v. Rines, 2 Sumner, 338; Beardsley v. Torrey, 4 Wash. C. C. 286; Ward v. Arredondo, 1 Paine, 410; In re Turner, 3 Wall. Jr. 260, Grier, J.; In re Girard, Ib., 263; Field v. Lownsdale, 1 Deady, 288; Fisk v. Union Pacific R. R. Co., 6 Blatchf. 362; s. c., 8 Blatchf. 243, 299; Dart v. Walker, 4 Daly (N. Y.), 188; Merwin v. Wexel, 49 How. (Pr.) Rep. (N. Y.), 115. The above cases discuss the right to and effect of successive removals by different defendants under various removal acts.

In Fallis v. McArthur, 1 Bond, 100 (1856), it was held that, where *one oint defendant* removed the suit (the other not being served), the plaintiff was entitled to process in the Federal court against the defendant who was not served with process in the State court at the time the cause was removed. In Field v. Lownsdale, *supra*, Deady, J., seems to be of a different opinion.   See opinion of Mr. Justice Nelson in Fisk v. Union Pacific R. R. Co., 8 Blatchf. 243 (1871); s. c., 8 Ib., 299; 6 Id. 362.

If a suit be brought by a citizen against several non-resident *joint debtors* in a state where the statute authorizes the plaintiff to proceed against the defendants served, and if he recover judgment, it may be enforced against the joint property of all, or the separate property of the defendants served, and the only defendants served are citizens of another state, such defendants are entitled to remove the cause, under the Judiciary Act, though the co-defendant not served does not join in the application. Davis v. Cook, 9 Nev. 134, (1874).

In an action for *joint indebtedness*, all the joint defendants, both under the act of July 27, 1866, and under that of March 2, 1867, must apply for the removal:—no one can remove under the act of 1866, unless a separate judgment can be rendered against him without the presence of the other defendants. Merwin v. Wexel, 49 How. (Pr.) Rep. 115.

[24] *Entering an appearance;* meaning of, construed and applied. Chatham Nat. Bank v. Merchants' Nat. Bank, 1 Hun. (N. Y.), 702, (Sup. Court, Special term 1874); Dart v. Cook, 9 Nev. 134 (1874); Hazard v. Durant *et al.*, 9 R. I. 602, 606; Hough v. West. Transp. Co., 1 Biss. 425, 1864; Sweeney v. Collin, 1 Dill. C. C. 73, Treat, J.; McBratney v. Usher, 1 Dill. C. C. 367; Webster v. Crothers, 1 Dill. C. C. 301. Other cases cited *infra*, see 13.

Under sec. 12 of the Judiciary Act the petition need not be verified. Sweeney v. Collin, 1 Dill. C. C. 73.

As to verification and mode of removal under other removal acts. Ib. Infra, secs. 12, 13, 14.

till; or if the defendants answered or submitted to the jurisdiction of the State court before applying for the removal; or if all the defendants (other than formal or nominal parties) did not apply for the transfer; or if the amount in dispute did not exceed $500—then, and in each of these cases, there could be no removal under the Judiciary Act.[25]

SECTION VI.

ACT OF JULY 27, 1866.

The act of July 27, 1866 (now Rev. Stat., sec. 639, subdivision 2), is the first act which allowed *part* of the defendants to remove a cause; but this right is given by the act only under specified and limited circumstances. Omitting the case of aliens, which is of unfrequent occurrence and presents little that is peculiar, the following conditions must co-exist to authorize a removal under this act:

1. The suit in the State court must be by a plaintiff who is a citizen of the state in which the suit is brought.

2. It must be against a citizen of the same state *and* a citizen of *another* state as defendants.

3. The *amount* in dispute must exceed the sum or value of $500, besides costs.

4. The removal must be applied for " before the trial or final hearing of the cause " in the State court.

These elements concurring, then the non-resident defendant (not the resident defendant), may have the cause removed, (not wholly), but only so far as relates to himself,·

[25] See *Infra*, secs. 8. 9, 13. 15. and cases cited.

There can be no removal under the Judiciary Act (Rev. Stats.. sec. 640. sub-division 1). if the plaintiff is an *alien*. Galvin v. Boutwell. 9 Blatchf. C. C. 470.

Federal jurisdiction dependent on *alienage*. Hinckley v. Byrne. 1 Deady. 224: Breedlove v. Nicolet. 7 Pet. 413: Wilson v. City Bank. 3 Sumner. 422: Montalet v. Murray. 4 Cranch. 46: Jackson v. Twentyman. 2 Pet. 136: *Infra*. sec. 12. *note*. Resident unnaturalized foreigners are deemed aliens. Baird v. Byrne, 3 Wall. Jr.: Lanz v. Randall. 3 Cent. L. J. 688: s. c.. 4 Dillon. C. C. *Indians* are not aliens. Karrahoo v. Adams. 1 Dill. C. C. 344.

provided also, it be a suit "brought for the purpose of restraining or enjoining him, or is a suit in which there can be
a *final determination* of the controversy, *so far as concerns
him*, without the presence of the other defendants as parties in the cause."[26]

[26] Construction and extent of application of the act of 1866. Hodg-
kins v. Hayes, 9 Abb. N. Y. Pr. (N. S.), 87; Darst v. Bates, 51 Ill. 439;
Stewart v. Mordecai, 40 Ga. 1.

In Cape Girardeau and State Line R. R. Co. v. Winston *et al.*, 4 Cent.
L. J. 127 (1877), before Dillon and Treat, JJ., the last named Judge was
strongly inclined to regard the act of 1866 as unconstitutional, and as
repealed by implication by the act of March 3, 1875,—the Circuit Judge
giving no opinion on these points, and both judges concurring in holding that, where in a suit brought in a State court by the plaintiff corporation *to set aside a deed of trust*, made by its officers and another corporation of *the same state*, a removal of the cause to the United States court
was sought by the surviving trustee in the deed of trust and one of the
bondholders under it, the latter corporation being a necessary party, and
no final or effectual determination of the case made by the bill being
possible without its presence, the petitioners could not have the cause
removed under the act of 1866 (Rev. Stat., sec. 639, clause 2), as to them.
See similar case, Gardner v. Brown, 21 Wall. 36, cited *infra*, sec. 9, note.

Construction of the act of 1866, as to cases in which there can
be a *final determination of the controversy* as to the portion of the defendants removing the cause, without the presence of the other defendants. See Bixby v. Couse, 8 Blatchf. 73; Peters v. Peters, 41 Ga. 242;
Allen v. Ryerson, 2 Dillon C. C. 501; Case of Sewing Machine Cos., 18
Wall. 583; s. c. below, 110 Mass. 70; Field v. Lamb, 1 Deady, 430;
Field v. Lownsdale, 1 Deady, 288 (1867). This last case holds that in
a suit to quiet title against *tenants in common*, one of the defendants, as
such tenant, may remove the case to the Federal court, under the act of
1866, if he is otherwise within its provisions.

In McGinnity v. White, 3 Dillon C. C. 350, it was held, under the circumstances, that one *copartner* might remove the cause as to himself
under the act of 1866.

The act of 1866 has no application to a case where one of the defendants is *an alien*, and the other defendants are citizens of *another state*,
and none of the defendants, or none who are served, are citizens of
the state in which the suit is brought. Davis v. Cook, 9 Nev. 134 (1874).

Under a *joint application* by two defendants, the removal may, under
the act of 1866, be granted to one and refused to the other. Dart v.
Walker, 4 Daly (N. Y.), 188.

Under the act of 1866, no *affidavit* of local prejudice is necessary, such
as is required by the act of 1867. Allen v. Ryerson, 2 Dillon C. C. 501.

As to *time and mode* of applying for removal under the act of 1866, see
infra, secs. 13, 14.

The express provision is that the suit as between the plaintiff (a citizen of the state), and the other defendant (also a citizen of the same state with the plaintiff), shall proceed in the State court nothwithstanding such removal to the Federal court. As between the plaintiff and the non-resident defendant (citizen of another state), the cause proceeds in the Federal court. It must be admitted that this is a singular result. The plaintiff's single action is thus split into two—one of which remains in the State court to be adjudged by it: the other goes to the Federal court to be adjudged by it. This act, it will be perceived, has no reference to cases in which *all* of the defendants are citizens of another state, (that being then provided for by section 12 of the Judiciary Act), nor any reference to the cases in which the plaintiffs are citizens of any other state than that in which the suit is brought. Its obvious purpose was to give a right of removal, in the cases and on the terms prescribed, to the non-resident citizen who was joined as a defendant with a resident citizen, when sued by a resident plaintiff.[27] It may be inferred that Congress doubted the power under the Constitution (art 3, sec. 2), to authorize the removal of the *whole* case, since part of the case provided for would be between citizens of the *same* state. We say this may be inferred, since otherwise we can scarcely conceive why it is that Congress would divide one case into two, and embarrass the parties with the inconvenience and additional expense resulting therefrom. Speaking of this act, Mr. Justice Clifford observes: " Considering the stringent conditions which are embodied therein, it is doubtful whether it will prove to be one of much practical value."[28] The necessity for this act grew out of the narrow construction early placed on the Judiciary Act, the embarrassments arising from which had been so long felt, and have finally led to the act of March 3, 1875. The ex-

[27] Bixby v. Couse, 8 Blatchf. 73; Allen v. Ryerson, 2 Dillon. 501; Field v. Lownsdale. 1 Deady, 288 (1867); Field v. Lamb. *Ib.* 430.
[28] Case of Sewing Machine Companies. 18 Wall. 553; s. c. below. 110 Mass. 70.

perience of the past should induce great caution in the
courts in applying to that act the rigid principles of the
early adjudications on the subject of Federal jurisdiction.[29]

SECTION VII.

ACT OF MARCH 2, 1867—" PREJUDICE OR LOCAL INFLUENCE."

We now come to the act of March 2, 1867.[30] It purports
to be an *amendment* to the act of July 27, 1866, last noticed, and it extends the right, in the cases therein provided
for, as well to *plaintiffs* as to defendants, but confines it to
such as are *non-residents* of the state in which the suit is
brought, and makes the ground of removal, not alone the
citizenship of the parties, but also prejudice or local influence.
The act provides, " That where a suit is now pending or
may hereafter be brought in any State court in which there
is a controversy between *a citizen of the state in which the
suit is brought* and a citizen of another state,   *   *   *
such citizen of another state, whether he be plaintiff or defendant, if he will make and file in such State court an affidavit that he has reason to believe and does believe that
from prejudice or local influence he will not be able to obtain justice in such State court," may have the cause removed to the Circuit court of the United States.   It will
be seen that, as to the plaintiff, this act follows the language
of section 11 of the Judiciary Act, and not of section 12 of
that act : the plaintiff may or may not be a resident of the
state where the suit is brought ; and the right of removal is
given to the non-resident party, be he the plaintiff or defendant.   Construing this act, Mr. Justice Miller, in Johnson v.
Monell,[31] says :

" *The only conditions necessary to the exercise of the right
of removal* under it are :

[29] See *infra* sec. 9 and note, and secs. 12 and 13.
[30] 14 Stats. at Large. 558; quoted *ante*, sec. 2, note.
[31] 1 Woolw. 390.

" 1. That the controversy shall be between a citizen of the state in which the suit is brought and a citizen of another state.

" 2. That the matter in dispute shall exceed the sum of five hundred dollars, exclusive of costs.

" 3. That the, party citizen of such other state shall file the required affidavit, stating, etc., the local prejudice.

" 4. Giving the requisite surety for appearing in the Federal court." * * * " Congress," adds this able judge, " intended to give the right in every case where the four requisites we have mentioned exist."

In the case just cited, the plaintiff was a citizen of Iowa, one defendant was a citizen of Nebraska, and the other of New York : but the last was not served with process and did not appear ; and it was held that the plaintiff was entitled, under the act of March 2, 1867, to have the case transferred from the State court to the United States court, after a verdict of the jury in the State court in his favor had been set aside by the court. This act, let it be noted, only applies where one of the parties is a citizen of the state in which the suit is brought, and the adverse party is a citizen of another state—in this respect conforming to the previous legislation on the subject.[32] This act undoubtedly grew out

[32] *Construction and extent of application of the act of 1867.—Policy and purpose* of the acts of 1866 and 1867, stated by Graves, C. J., in Crane v. Reeder, 28 Mich. 527 (1874) : by Potter, J., in Hazard v. Durant *et al.*, 9 R. I. 602 (1868) : by Blatchford, J., in Fisk v. Union Pacific R. R. Co., 6 Blatchf. 362: by Gray, C. J., in Galpin v. Critchlow, 112 Mass. 339 (1873).

The act of 1867 (Rev. Stats. sec. 639, cl. 3) does not apply, where the cause of removal is *alienage*, but is *limited to citizens:* Crane v. Reeder, 28 Mich. 527, (1874) ; Davis v. Cook, 9 Nev. 134. (1874).

Under act of 1867 the *whole suit* is to be removed. Sewing Machine Cos.' Case, 18 Wall. 553; s. c. below. 110 Mass. 81: Cooke v. State Nat. Bank, 52 N. Y. 96, (1873) ; s. c. below. 1 Lansing. 494. And *all the defendants*, not nominal or merely formal parties, must apply for the removal. Bixby v. Couse (Blatchford, J.), 8 Blatchf. 73, (1870) : Cooke v. State Nat. Bank. 1 Lansing (N. Y.). 494; s. c., 52 N. Y. 96, (1873). As to who are nominal or formal parties, see *ante.*

Parties—Citizenship under act of 1867. In the leading case on this stat-

of the condition of affairs in the Southern states after the
War of the Rebellion, and was intended to afford to
plaintiffs who had resorted to the State court the right

ute, entitled in the report the Sewing Machine Companies' Case, it was
decided that an action *ex contractu*, by a plaintiff who was a citizen of the
state in which the suit was brought, against two defendants, citizens of
other states, *and* a third defendant, a citizen of the *same state as the
plaintiff*, was not removable under the act of 1867, upon the petition of
the two non-resident defendants, (18 Wall. 553); and the same principle
was re-asserted in a subsequent case, where the removal of the *whole
suit*, under the act of 1867, was sought, and not of the suit as to the non-
resident defendants under the act of 1866. Vannevar v. Bryant, 21 Wall.
41; Case v. Douglas, 1 Dillon. 299; Johnson v. Monell (change of residence), 1 Woolw. 390; Bixby v. Couse, 8 Blatchf. 73 (1870); Florence
etc. Co. v. Grover & Baker etc. Co., 110 Mass. 70, affirmed 18 Wall. 553.

In the case of Burnham v. Chicago, Dubuque & Minnesota Railroad
Co. *et al.*, the Circuit court of the United States, for the district of Iowa,
May term, 1876 (Miller and Dillon, JJ.), decided the following: A foreclosure suit by trustees in a railway mortgage, who are citizens of *Massachusetts*, was commenced in one of the State courts in Iowa, against
the debtor company (which is an *Iowa* corporation), making an *Illinois*
and an *Indiana* corporation, each of which claimed liens upon the property, also defendants to the bill; this suit, after all of the defendants had
answered, was removed, in 1876, to the Circuit court of the United States
for the district of Iowa, upon the petition of the *plaintiffs* under the act
of 1867. Rev. Stat., sec. 639, sub-division 3. The debtor corporation
moved to remand the same to the State court, because *all* of the defendants were not citizens of *the state in which the suit was brought*. Held, inasmuch as the case was one clearly within sec. 2, of the act of March 3,
1875, in respect of removals, and the controversy, one in relation to the
priority of liens between citizens of different states, that the Circuit
court had jurisdiction, and that it should not be remanded. See Beery
v. Irick, 22 Gratt. 484.

Under the act of 1867, where *non-resident and resident plaintiffs* are
joined, the non-resident plaintiffs can not remove the case wholly or as
to themselves. All the plaintiffs must be citizens of the state in which
the suit is brought. Bliss v. Rawson, 43 Ga. 181 (1871). See Stewart
v. Mordecai, 40 Ga. 1; Bryant v. Scott, 67 N. C. 391 (1872); Case v.
Douglas, 1 Dillon C. C. 299.

In Sands v. Smith, 1 Abb. U. S. 368, s. c., 1 Dillon. 290, it was held
that, under the act of 1867, a non-resident plaintiff might remove a suit
against a citizen of the state in which it was brought *and* a citizen of a
third state who had voluntarily appeared, as to all the defendants. This
seems to be right in view of the act of 1839; but some doubt is thrown
upon the case by the reference to it in the Sewing Machine Cos.' case, 18
Wall. 553.

to transfer their suits to the Federal courts.³³ This is the first act that in any event extended the right to a *plaintiff* to leave the forum he had voluntarily chosen, and in this respect was an entire departure from all the previous legislation. It is not so difficult to justify the act in this respect, even if it was intended to be permanent, as it is to sustain the provision that this removal may be had, on filing the general affidavit of prejudice or local influence, the truth of which can not be contested or inquired into, "at *any time* before trial or final hearing of the suit." This provision occasions delay, and is often resorted to for that purpose. But the act of 1867 has been expressly adjudged by the Supreme Court to be constitutional,³⁴ and Congress has not, in our judgment, repealed or modified it. There is no express repeal, and it is not, according to the better view, repealed by implication by the act of March 3, 1875, next to be noticed.³⁵

In passing for the present from this act, we direct attention to Mr. Justice Miller's vindication of it. He says : " I do not join in the condemnation of the act of 1867. It does not allow the removal solely on the ground of citizenship. It requires the requisite citizenship to exist, and in addition thereto requires the existence of prejudice or local influence to be shown by affidavit. In this respect the policy of that act is not unlike that which prevails in perhaps all the states in regard to the change of venue from one county, or one

Case v. Douglas (citizenship of plaintiffs who are copartners). 1 Dill. C. C. 299; Cooke v. State Nat. Bank (all the defendants must unite). 1 Lansing. N. Y. 494; s. c.. 52. N. Y. 96 (1873); Washington etc. R. R. Co. v. Alexandria etc. R. R. Co.. (act of 1867 does not repeal act of 1866). 19 Gratt. (Va.). 562 (1870); Fields v. Lamb (as to repeal, etc.) 1 Deady, 430; Beecher v. Gillett (removal by substituted defendant). 1 Dillon C. C. 308; Johnson v. Monell (time of removal—change of residence), 1 Woolw. 390.

Decisions concerning the *affidavit* required by this act, see *infra*, sec. 14.

³³Gaines v. Fuentes, U. S. Sup. Court. Oct. term, 1875. 3 Cent. L. J. 371; s. c.. 2 Otto. 10.

³⁴Chicago & N. W. Railway Co. v. Whitton's Admr. 13 Wall. 270.

³⁵*Infra*, sec. 8.

judicial district, to another. Johnson v. Monell, 1 Woodw.
390. The object in each case is to secure an impartial tribunal, and the Federal courts are not courts for non-residents
more than for residents, and no injustice is done to the latter
to be compelled there to litigate controversies which they
may have with citizens of other states." [36]

SECTION VIII.

ACT OF MARCH 3, 1875.

We now reach the act of March 3, 1875 (19 Stats. at
Large, 470), entitled " an act to determine the jurisdiction
of the Circuit courts of the United States, and to regulate
the removal of causes from State courts, and for other
purposes."

The first section of the act relates to the *original jurisdiction* of the Circuit court, civil and criminal, greatly enlarg-
ing the jurisdiction in civil cases, and conferring a jurisdiction concurrent with the courts of the several states, using
for this purpose the language of the article of the Constitution (art. 3, sec. 2), which defines and limits the judicial
power of the general government. The civil jurisdiction,
as there conferred, is given in certain specified cases by
reason of the *subject-matter*, irrespective of the citizenship
of the parties, and in other cases by reason of *citizenship*,
irrespective of the subject-matter. It is material to notice
the clause giving jurisdiction on the ground of citizenship.
It removes the limitation prescribed by the Judiciary Act
and by the prior removal acts, requiring one of the parties
to the suit, that is, either the plaintiffs or the defendants, to
be citizens of the state where the suit is brought. On the
contrary, the act of March 3, 1875, confers jurisdiction of
all suits of a civil nature, over $500, in which there shall be
a controversy between citizens of different states, without

[36] Farmers' etc. Trust Co. v. Maquillan. 3 Dillon. 379. 381.

requiring any of the parties to be citizens of the state in which the suit is brought. The second section of the act relates to removals [note to see 2, *ante*] ; and as to the suits which may be removed, it follows the language of the first section. So that it is true, in general, that any cause may, at the proper time and in the prescribed mode, be removed from the State court to the Circuit court of the United States, which, by reason of either its subject-matter or the citizenship of the parties, might have been instituted originally in the Federal court.

The act of 1875 on the one hand adds to or enlarges the classes of cases that may be removed, and on the other hand restricts the time in which the removal must be applied for within narrower limits than the acts of 1866 and 1867. The required amount or value is the same as before, *i. e.*, it must exceed $500, exclusive of costs. In all previous legislation, the right of removal, where citizenship is the ground, is limited to the non-resident citizen, whereas in the act of 1875 it is given to "*either party*," and in certain circumstances to either one or more of the plaintiffs or defendants. This is a radical change of policy.

An analysis of the second section of the act shows that in respect of *subject-matter*, without reference to citizenship, it gives the right of removal of "any suit of a civil nature at law or in equity," involving over $500, (1) arising under the Constitution, or laws or treaties of the United States ; or (2) in which the United States shall be plaintiff or petitioner. And in respect of *citizenship*, without regard to subject-matter, it gives the right of removal (1) in any suit "*in which there shall be a controversy between citizens of different states:* or (2) a controversy between citizens of the same state claiming lands under grants of different states ; or (3) a controversy between citizens of a state and foreign states, citizens, or subjects."

In respect of the *time* in which the removal must be applied for, the provision is that the petition therefor must be filed in the State court "before or at the term at which the

cause *could be first tried*, and before the trial thereof."
The decisions under the acts of 1866 and 1867 as to removals after one trial had and a new trial granted, which
will be alluded to hereafter, may not be and probably are
not applicable under the act of 1875.[37]

Many questions of great importance arise under this act,
among which we may mention in this place the question how
far it repeals, if at all, the 12th section of the Judiciary Act,
the act of 1866 and the act of 1867, or rather these several
acts as substantially embodied in the 639th section of the
Revised Statutes. There is no express repeal in the act of
1875 (see section 10), of any specified previous acts, the repeal being only of " all acts and parts of acts in conflict
with the provisions of this act." It would seem that sub
division one of sec. 639, Revised Statutes, (12th section of
the Judiciary Act), is practically repealed by reason of being merged in the more enlarged right given by the act of
1875. If, however, a case should arise which could be removed under this provision, but which could not be removed
under the act of 1875, the former would be held to be still
subsisting. If a liberal construction shall be, and can con-
stitutionally be, given to the latter portion of section 2 of
the act of 1875, the above remark as to repeal may possi-
bly apply, except as to time, to sub-division *second* of section 639 of the Revised Statutes, corresponding to the act
of 1866. But the better view, probably, is that the act of
1866 is not repealed by the act of 1875; that is to say, if a
case is brought within its provisions, it may still be removed
thereunder, and cases may arise of such a nature, that they
would fall within the act of 1866, and not within that of
1875; in which event the latter act should not be held to
repeal by implication the former. The *third* sub-division of
that section (corresponding to the act of 1867) is broader
than the act of 1875, provides for a class of cases not provided for by that act, and while the point is not free of

---

[37] See *infra*, sec. 13. as to *time* of applying for the removal under the
act of 1875; *infra*, sec. 14. as to *mode* of effecting the removal.

doubt, the true view seems to be that at all events this portion of the 639th section remains unrepealed. This has been decided to be so in the 8th circuit by Mr. Justice Miller, and generally in the courts of that circuit, and so far as we are advised, by the Circuit courts elsewhere.

Concerning the nature of the suits that may be removed under the act of 1875, perhaps the true view is, that it contemplates the removal of the *whole suit*, and not, like the act of 1866, of part of a suit. This has been thus held in the 7th circuit.[38] If, therefore, the main and essential controversy is between citizens of the same state, a non-resident defendant interested in a collateral branch of the case can not remove it under the act of March 3, 1875.[39]

One of the most important questions which arises under the act of 1875 is, whether the Federal judicial power as conferred and limited by the Constitution can, by reason of *citizenship*, extend to a case in which some of the necessary defendants are citizens of the *same state* with the plaintiffs or some of the plaintiffs. Expressions may, perhaps, be found in opinions of the Supreme Court construing the 11th and 12th sections of the Judiciary Act and the removal acts of 1866 and 1867, which deny, or would seem to deny, that under the Constitution the Federal judicial power extends on the ground of citizenship to cases where any of the defendants in interest are citizens of the same state with the plaintiffs, although some of the defendants may be citizens

---

[38] Chicago v. Gage (Blodgett. J.). 8 Chicago Legal News. 49 (1875) ; s. c., 6 Bissell. 467 ; Osgood v. Chicago etc. R. R. Co. (Drummond. J.), 7 Ch. Legal News. 241 ; s. c., 6 Bissell. 330. In Ellerman v. New Orleans etc. R. R. Co., 2 Woods. C. C. 120 (1875). Mr. Circuit Judge Woods held that, under the act of 1875, there may be a removal of that part of a cause which concerns the original parties, notwithstanding a statute of the state may declare that the trial as to certain other parties can not be separated from the trial of the main cause,—leaving the latter issue in the State court. But the point did not require much consideration, for the reason that the latter parties had disclaimed and had no such interest in the suit or relative to it, as to defeat the right of removal.

[39] Chicago v. Gage (Blodgett, J.). 8 Chicago Legal News. 49. (1875) ; s. c., 6 Bissell. 467.

of other states than the one of which the plaintiff is a citizen. But all the legislation previous to the act of 1875 was such, that the Supreme Court was not necessarily obliged to decide this question ; and it is in our judgment properly to be considered as still open. It will be extremely embarrassing and unfortunate, if the Supreme Court shall feel constrained to assign such narrow limits to the Constitution. Looking at the purpose in the grant of the Federal judicial power in the Constitution, and the benefits which are felt to flow from the exercise of this jurisdiction, and the embarrassments which would result from a close and rigid construction of the Constitution in this regard, we think the Supreme Court would be justified in holding that a case does not cease to be one between citizens of different states, because one or some of the defendants are citizens of the same state with the plaintiffs or some of the plaintiffs, provided the other defendants are citizens of another or other states. If the substantial controversy is wholly between citizens of the same state, it is not, and can not become, one of Federal cognizance ; but if the real litigation is between citizens of different states, the case is within the constitutional grant of Federal judicial power, notwithstanding some of the adversary parties may happen to be citizens of the same state with some of the plaintiffs.

The case of Lockhart v. Horn, 1 Woods, C. C. R. 628, 634 (1871), arising under a former act, contains an expression of the opinion of Mr. Justice Bradley concerning the constitutional question above mentioned. In conformity with the accepted construction prior to that act he held, that the Circuit court has no jurisdiction of a cause in which the plaintiff and part only of the defendants were citizens of the *same* state, although they answer without objecting to the jurisdiction. He says : " Were this an original question, I should say that the fact of a common state citizenship existing between the complainants and a part only of the defendants, provided the other defendants were citizens of the proper state, would not oust the court of jurisdiction. .

It certainly would not under the Constitution. The case would still be a controversy between citizens of different states.[40] [The act of 1875 uses the language of the Constitution, it will be remembered.] " But the strict construction put by the courts upon the Judiciary Act," he continues, " is conclusive against the jurisdiction ; and I am

[40] See. on this subject, case of Sewing Machine Cos.. 18 Wall. 553, affirming s. c.. 110 Mass. 70. 80; New Orleans v. Winter. 1 Wheat. 91 (1816); Woods v. Davis. 18 How. 467; Hepburn v. Ellzey. 2 Cranch. 445; Strawbridge v. Curtiss. 3 Cranch. 267.

In the case of Bryant v. Rich. 106 Mass. 192. (s. c. in U. S. Sup. Court, under name of Vannevar v. Bryant, 21 Wall. 41). Chief Justice Gray says *arguendo :* " Five of the nine defendants in this case, as well as the plaintiff, are citizens of this commonwealth; and the *courts of the United States are not authorized by the Constitution* to take jurisdiction, so far as it depends upon the citizenship of the parties, of suits between citizens of the same state, but only of suits between citizens of different states, or between a citizen and an alien, and can therefore have no jurisdiction (except when it grows out of the subject-matter) of an action in which any of the plaintiffs and of the defendants, who are real parties in interest, by or against whom relief is sought, are citizens of the same state. Const. of U. S.. art. 3. § 2; Strawbridge v. Curtiss, 3 Cranch. 267: New Orleans v. Winter. 1 Wheat. 91; Wood v. Davis. 18 How. 467: Tuckerman v. Bigelow. 21 Law Reporter, 208; Wilson v. Blodgett, 4 McLean, 363."

An examination of the cases here cited will show that they turn upon the language of the Judiciary Act. and not on the Constitution. So, in the very recent case of Ober v. Gallagher. (U. S. Sup. Court. Oct. Term, 1876). Chief Justice Waite says, *arguendo,* that if " an *indispensable party was a citizen of the same state with the plaintiff,* the jurisdiction would be defeated, because the controversy would not be between citizens of different states, and thus *not within the judicial power of the United States, as defined by the Constitution.* The decisions to this effect are numerous: Hagan v. Walker. 14 How. 36; Shields v. Barrow. 17 How. 141; Clearwater v. Meredith. 21 How. 492; Insbach v. Farwell, 1 Blatchf. 571; Barnes v. Baltimore City, 6 Wall. 286; Jones v. Andrews. 10 Wall. 332; Commercial and R. R. Bank of Vicksburg v. Slocomb. 14 Pet. 65. In Louisville R; R. Co. v. Letson, 2 How. 497. it is also distinctly stated (p. 556), that the act of 1839 was passed exclusively with an intent to rid the courts of the decision in the case of Strawbridge v. Curtiss. 3 Cranch, 267, which, with that of the Bank v. Deveaux, 5 Cranch. 84. had · never been satisfactory to the bar.' " But the cases here cited did not *necessarily* involve an inquiry or decision as to the extent of the constitutional point of judicial power as respects controversies between *citizens of different states.*

bound by it. Nevertheless, the case is such that the complainant may dismiss his bill as to the obnoxious defendants and hold it as to the others. I will permit him to do so. This should be allowed in all cases where the objection is not made *in limine*."

The judicial power of the United States, as conferred by the Constitution, extends " *to all cases arising under the Constitution and Laws of the United States,*" whether they are pending in the State or Federal tribunals. The act of March 3, 1875, both in prescribing the original jurisdiction of the Circuit courts of the United States, and in describing the class of cases which may be removed into the Circuit courts from the State courts, follows the language of the Constitution. It is therefore important to know, *what is a case arising under the Constitution or Laws of the United States.* The question has been frequently before the Supreme Court of the United States, and some of the leading judgments are cited in the note.[41] " A case in law or equity consists of the right of the one party, as well as the other, and may be truly said to arise under the Constitution or a law of the United States, whenever its correct decision depends upon a right construction of either."[42] " Nor is it," says Mr. Justice Swayne, " any objection, that questions are involved which are not all of a Federal character. If one of the latter exist, if there be a single such ingredient in the mass, it is sufficient. That element is decisive upon

---

[41] Martin v. Hunter's Lessees, 1 Wheat. 314: Cohens v. Virginia, 6 Wheat. 264; Osborn v. Bank of U. S., 9 Wheat. 821; United States v. Peters, 5 Cranch. 115: Ableman v. Booth, 21 How. 506: Meserole v. Union Paper Collar Co., 6 Blatchf. 356; Freeman v. Howe, 24 How. 450; Murdock v. Memphis (full discussion), 20 Wall. 591: The Mayor v. Cooper, 6 Wall. 247: Murray v. Patric, 5 Blatchf. 343: Claflin v. Houseman (U. S. Sup. Court. Oct. Term. 1876). 9 Ch. Legal News. 105; s. c., 3 Cent. L. J. 803; N. Y. Life Ins. Co. v. Hendren (U. S. Sup. Court, Oct. Term, 1875). 8 Ch. Legal News. 385: Ames v. Colorado Central R. R. Co.. 9 Ch. Legal News. 132: s. c., 3 Cent. L. J. 815.   See *ante*, sec. 2 and note. and cases cited under the acts of 1833 and July 27, 1868 (Rev. Stats., sec. 640).
[42] Per Marshall. C. J.. in Cohens v. Virginia, 6 Wheat. 379.

the subject of jurisdiction,"[43] whether it exists in favor of the plaintiff or the defendant.

But there must be some question actually involved in the case, depending for its determination upon the correct construction of the Constitution, or some law of Congress, or some treaty of the United States, in order to sustain the Federal jurisdiction under the clause under consideration, namely, " suits arising under the Constitution, or laws or treaties of the United States." Accordingly, a case relating to the title to land is not one of Federal jurisdiction, although the title may be originally derived under an act of Congress, if no question arises, or is raised, as to the validity or operative effect of the act of Congress, and the rights of the parties depend upon State statutes or the general principles of law.[44]

[43] The Mayor v Cooper. 6 Wall. 252; Connor v. Scott (West. Dist. Ark.. Parker, J.) 3 Cent. L. J. 305.

When a case involves the construction of the *bankrupt act*. it may be removed to the Federal court, under the act of March 3. 1875. Connor v. Scott (West. Dist. Ark., Parker, J.), 3 Cent. L. J. 305 (1876); Payson v. Dietz (removal by assignee in bankruptcy, on ground of citizenship), 5 Ch. Legal News, 434; Trafton v. Nougues (as to removal of suits in relation to mining claims), 13 Pacific Law Rep. 49; s. c., 4 Cent. L. J. 228, cited *infra*.

[44] McStay v. Friedman, 92 U. S. R. (2 Otto). 723; Romie v. Casanova, 91 U. S. R. (1 Otto), 380; Trafton v. Nougues (Dist. Cal.. Sawyer, Circuit Judge), 13 Pacific Law Rep. 49 (1877); s. c. 4 Cent. L. J. 228. The learned Circuit Judge. in the case last cited, upon a review of certain decisions of the Supreme Court of the United States. arrives at the following conclusions: 1. Only suits involving rights depending upon a disputed construction of the Constitution and Laws of the United States can be transferred from the State to the National courts. under the clause " arising under the Constitution and Laws of the United States." of section 2 of the Act to determine the jurisdiction of the United States courts, passed March 3d, 1875. 2. Where the only questions to be litigated in suits to determine the right to mining claims are, as to what are the local laws, rules. regulations and customs by which the rights of the parties are governed. and whether the parties have in fact conformed to such local laws and customs, the courts of the United States have no jurisdiction of the cases under the provisions of the Act giving jurisdiction in suits " arising under the Constitution and Laws of the United States."

3

SECTION IX.

NATURE OF SUITS THAT MAY BE REMOVED UNDER THE SEV
ERAL REMOVAL ACTS—PRACTICE AS TO REPLEADER.

We are prepared after this general survey of the subject
to consider in detail other important topics belonging to it.
*As to nature of suits that may be removed under the acts
we have been reviewing.* The language of section 639 of
the Revised Statutes is " any suit   *   *   *   wherein the

Requisites of petitions to transfer causes from State to Federal court
under the above clause of section 3 of the act of March 3, 1875, see *post*,
sec. 14.

Two new and interesting points under the act of 1875 were ruled by
Mr. Justice Davis and Judge Treat at the July Term, 1876, of the Circuit
Court of the U. S., for the Southern District of Illinois. Mr. Robert E.
Williams, of Bloomington, Illinois, of counsel in the causes, has thus
stated the facts and substance of the decisions:

Turner Bros., citizens of New York, filed a bill against the Indianapolis, Bloomington & Western R. R. Co., the Farmers' Loan and Trust
Co. *et al.*, in the State court, and a receiver was appointed. There were
three mortgages on the road—in the first two, the Farmers' Loan
and Trust Co. is trustee—in the other, an individual is trustee. Turner
Bros. claimed to be bondholders of bonds under each of the mortgages,
and also to be floating or unsecured creditors to a large amount. The
receiver, it was claimed, was appointed by collusion between the parties.
As soon as the Farmers' Loan and Trust Co. learned of the appointment
of the receiver, it appeared in the State court, answered the bill, and filed
a cross-bill to foreclose the two mortgages, and then filed a petition and
bond to remove the case to the Federal court under the act of 1875.
Turner Bros., the complainants in the bill, are citizens of New York, and
the F. L. & T. Co. is a citizen of New York; but Turner Bros. were
not, it was claimed, necessary parties to the litigation. A motion was
made to remand to the State court for want of jurisdiction in the Federal court, as Turner Bros. and the F. L. & T. Co. were all citizens of
New York. After full argument and consideration, Mr. Justice Davis
announced the opinion both of himself and Judge Treat, in which he
said that there was not a doubt that the case was properly transferred,
and that the Federal court had jurisdiction. In substance he remarked,
They, Turner Bros., sued in a double aspect, as bondholders and unsecured creditors. As bondholders their bill did not in any way charge on
the trustee in either of the mortgages an inability or unwillingness to
act, and all of the trustees were in fact parties and trying to enforce the
trust; therefore, as bond creditors, they, Turner Bros., were not necessary

amount in dispute, * * exceeds the sum or value of five hundred dollars." The language of the act of 1875 (sec. 2) is " any suit of a civil nature at law or in equity." Although the language is different, the meaning is doubtless the same. It does not extend to *criminal* prosecutions, being

parties. As floating-debt creditors there was no controversy between the Turner Bros. and the trustee in the mortgages—as, of course, the mortgage took precedence of the floating debts; that as to the floating debts the only controversy was between the creditors and the debtor, the Railroad Co.; that, therefore, the principal controversy was between the trustees in the mortgages (the F. L. & T. Co.) and the corporation, and that the claim of Turner Bros. for their unsecured debt was improperly introduced into the case, and could not oust the Federal court of its rightful jurisdiction over the main controversy between the mortgagor and the mortgagees; but even if Turner Bros. as unsecured creditors had a right to be parties at all, their right was only to the surplus after payment of all mortgages, and their controversy was merely an incident to the main controversy about the mortgages, and that the intention of Congress, as plainly expressed in the act of March 3, 1875, was that, where the main controversy in a case was between citizens of different states, it was removable and carried with it all the incidents, and that a mere incident would not prevent the case from being removed.

The other case was this: A road in the southern part of the state had made a mortgage to the Farmers' Loan & Trust Co. A judgment creditor, by collusion with the Railroad Co., filed a bill and got a receiver appointed by the State court, making no defendant to the bill but the Railroad Co. It was claimed that this was done with the intent to obtain an undue advantage over the bondholders. As soon as the F. L. & T. Co. learned of it, it applied to the State court to be permitted to become a party defendant. It presented a sworn petition setting up its rights as trustee, and asking leave to be made a defendant, and with it filed an answer to the bill and a cross-bill to foreclose the mortgage. The State court refused to admit the F. L. & T. Co. as a defendant, saying it could not make such an order in vacation. The F. L. & T. Co. at once filed in the State court its papers—that is, its petition, answer and cross-bill, and a petition and bond to remove the case to the Federal court, and brought the record to the Federal court. There was no question about the citizenship of the parties; but the question was, as the F. L. & T. Co. was not made a defendant by the bill, and the State court had refused to make an order admitting it as a party, was it, the F. L. & T. Co., such a party within the meaning of the act of Congress as could file the petition and bond for removal? The F. L. & T. Co. contended that it was, as it was absolutely a necessary party to the litigation, and had done all it could to become a party; and if the State court could refuse to admit it as a party, it could nullify the act of Congress and leave the mortgagee without remedy.

limited to suits of a *civil* nature.[45] All cases which fall
within the ordinary notion of an action at law on contract
or for tort, or of a suit in equity, are undoubtedly em-
braced by the language. Speaking of the nature of suits
which may be removed under the 12th section of the Judiciary Act (Revised Statutes, § 639, sub-division 1), Mr.
Chief Justice Chase in West v. Aurora,[46] said: " A suit
removable from a State court must be a suit regularly commenced by a citizen of the state in which the suit is
brought, by process served upon the defendant who is a citizen of another state, and who, if he does not elect to remove, is bound to submit to the jurisdiction of the State
court." This language is, perhaps, too broad to be strictly
applicable to all cases, since suits have been held removable, and properly so we think, which were not " regularly
commenced " in the State court on process issued from it.[47]

Mr. Justice Davis decided that it was an absolutely necessary party, and
that, as it had done all it could to become a party and had been wrongfully refused the right by the State court, it was a party for the purpose
of removing the case, and that the case was rightfully removed.

[45] See Rison v. Cribbs, 1 Dillon, 181, 184; Green v. United States, 9
Wall. 655.

[46] 6 Wall. 139 (1867).

[47] Patterson v. Boom Co., 3 Dillon, 465. In the case last cited it was
held that a suit pending in a State court, between a land owner and an
incorporated company seeking to appropriate his private property under
the right of eminent domain, where the question to be tried is the value
of such land, is *a suit of such a nature as may be removed* to the Federal
court, although the proceeding in its inception was an appraisement by
commissioners appointed under the charter of the company.

What is an *original suit* which may be removed, and what is a mere
supplement or sequence of a former suit and decree in the State court,
is illustrated by the case of Hatch v. Preston, 1 Biss. 19 (1853), Drummond, J. See West v. Aurora, *supra.*

Plaintiff sued at law in the State court on a policy, and while it was
pending, filed a bill in equity to reform it. Held, that the defendant
might remove the equity suit—that being an *original suit* within the
meaning of sec. 12 of the Judiciary Act, and not simply a suit ancillary
to or in aid of the suit at law. Charter Oak Fire Ins. Co. v. Star Ins.
Co., (Nelson, J.), 6 Blatchf. 208 (1868).

A *garnishee or trustee*, holding property or credits of the principal defendant and joined as defendant for that purpose, was held by the Su-

The case of West v. Aurora, *supra*, is interesting as illustrating a class of questions which arise in respect of removals in consequence of the practice in the code states of mingling, or rather uniting legal and equitable relief in the *same* suit. In brief the case was this : The plaintiff sued the city of Aurora in the State court on coupons. The city made certain defenses, and by an additional answer prayed an injunction to restrain plaintiff from proceeding in any suit on the coupons, and from transferring them, and for a decree that the same be canceled and delivered up. Upon the filing of this additional answer the plaintiff discontinued his suit, and assuming that he was a defendant to the case made in the additional answer, and that this was a new suit against him, applied to remove the cause into the Federal court, under section 12 of the Judiciary Act. The Supreme Court held the case not removable and observed : " The filing of the additional paragraphs did not make a new suit within the meaning of the Judiciary Act. They were in the nature of defensive pleas, coupled with a prayer for injunction and general relief. This, if allowed by the code of Indiana (as it was), might give them, in some sense, the character of an original suit, but not such as could be re-'moved from the jurisdiction of the State court," under the Judiciary Act which gives the right " only to a defendant who promptly avails himself of it at the time of appearance ;" but here the plaintiffs had " submitted themselves, by voluntarily resorting to the State court, to its jurisdiction in its whole extent."[48] Some of the cases illustrative of the nature of suits that may be removed are cited in a note.[49]

perior Court of Judicature of New Hampshire as not within the removal act of 1866. and hence could not have a transfer of the case as to himeslf. leaving the cause as between the principal parties in the State court. Weeks v. Billings. 55 N. H. 371 (1875).

[48] See *infra*. sec. 13.

[49] *Suits by attachment* may be removed. Barney v. Globe Bank. 5 Blatchf. 107 ; Sayles v. N. W. Ins. Co.. 2 Curtis C. C. 212. And *ejectment* actions. *Ex parte* Turner. 3 Wall. Jr. 258 : Torrey v. Beardsley. 4 Wash. C. C. R. 242 : Allin v. Robinson. 1 Dillon. 119 ; *Ex parte* Girard.

Where the case made by the pleadings in the State court is in its nature a *law action*, it must, when removed to the 3 Wall. Jr. 263 (1868). Grier. J. And in *replevin*. Beecher v. Gillett. 1 Dillon. 308; Dennistoun v. Draper. 5 Blatchf. 336. And a *bill in equity* to reform an insurance policy. Charter Oak Co. v. Star Ins. Co., 6 Blatchf. 208. And a *special statutory proceeding* in the nature of a *chancery remedy* to confirm a tax title. Parker v. Overman. 18 How. 137; s. c. Hempstead. 692.

A proceeding to appropriate private property for public use. which at the time the removal was applied for had assumed the shape of an action at law regularly docketed in the State court, to be tried and determined as other cases. and judgment entered accordingly. is such a *suit* as may be removed. Patterson v. Boom Co., 3 Dillon. 465.

Suit in a State court by strangers, the object of which is *to annul a will* and to recall the decree by which it was allowed to probate. is in effect a suit in equity, and may be removed to the Circuit court under the act of March 2. 1867. Gaines v. Fuentes, (Oct. Term, 1875, U. S. Sup. Court. 3 Cent. L. J. 371; s. c. 2 Otto. 10, overruling s. c.. 25 La. An. 85). distinguished from Broderick's Will case. 21 Wall. 503. and proceedings to probate wills. Fouvergne v. New Orleans. 18 How. 470.

Under the legislation of Massachusetts in respect to the *establishment of claims against the estates of deceased persons*. which provides for the examination, by Commissioners of the Probate Court, of all claims of creditors against the estate, and for the allowance or rejection by the Commissioners of each claim, and which requires a statement of the amount allowed on each claim and a list of claims finally allowed. with a provision for an appeal by either party to a Superior court, which shall be tried as in an action at law prosecuted in the usual manner. except that no execution shall be awarded, it was held that such a claim. pending on appeal in the Superior court from the decision of commissioners appointed by the Probate court, could not be removed to the Circuit court of the United States under the act of 1867. Du Vivier v. Hopkins. 116 Mass. 125 (1874). This decision was rested upon two general grounds: 1. The claim against an estate is not such a *suit* as is contemplated by the removal acts of Congress; the Supreme Judicial Court of Massachusetts being of opinion that the jurisdiction of the State courts over the entire proceedings for the settlement of the estate is exclusive of the Federal courts; [but see Craigie v. McArthur. 9 Ch. Legal News. 156; s. c.. 4 Cent. L. J. 237; s. c., 15 Al. Law J. 121; s. c.. 4 Dillon C. C.: Payne v. Hook, 7 Wall. 425; s. c., 14 Wall. 252]; that nothing less than the whole cause can be removed, while here was an attempt, in the opinion of the Court. to remove part of the proceeding; that on the removal of a cause, where the right exists. the jurisdiction of the State court ceases and the Federal court must execute its own judgment. and can not after judgment remand the cause for any purpose, or transmit a certificate of its judgment to the State court, it not being an appellate tribunal, but a court of co-ordinate and independent jurisdiction: and

Federal court, proceed as such, and may do so (where the action is a purely legal one), although it is brought in the

here the Federal court could not issue execution on its judgment or certify the same to the State court. 2. The application could not be made in the appellate court, but under the act of Congress must be made in the court of original jurisdiction before final judgment; and here the decision of the Commissioners of the Probate Court would be final, unless modified by the State appellate court. The view of the Supreme Judicial Court of Massachusetts that a claim against the estate of a deceased person is not, under the statute of that state, such a *suit* as falls within the provision of the removal acts of Congress, is doubtless correct, at least while the proceeding is in the Probate court; but on the appeal of the creditor or executor the statute provided, that the supposed creditor shall file a written statement of his claim, in the nature of a declaration, "and like proceedings shall thereupon be had in the pleadings, trial and determination of the case as in an action at law prosecuted in the usual manner, except that no execution shall be awarded." This would seem to assimilate the case in the appellate court to an ordinary suit; but if so, the difficulty was that the application for the removal was not made before the final trial in the court of original jurisdiction as required by the act. Further as to the Federal jurisdiction in respect to suits concerning the settlement of estates of deceased persons, the probate of wills, etc., see Mallett v. Dexter, 1 Curtis C. C. R. 178. Compare with Payne v. Hook, 7 Wall. 425; Williams v. Benedict, 8 How. 107; Vaughan v. Northup, 15 Pet. 1; Pratt v. Northam, 5 Mason C. C. 95; Gaines v. Fuentes, 2 Otto. 10, overruling s. c., 25 La. Ann. 85; Tarver v. Tarver, 9 Pet. 174; Gaines v. Chew, 2 How. 619, 650; Gaines v. New Orleans, 6 Wall. 642; Gaines v. Hennen, 24 How. 553; Fuentes v. Gaines, 1 Woods C. C. 112, where Mr. Justice Bradley reviews previous cases of Mrs. Gaines in the Supreme Court; Case of Broderick's Will, 21 Wall. 503; Burts v. Loyd, 45 Ga. 104; Hargroves v. Redd, 43 Ga. 143; Craigie v. McArthur, 9 Ch. Legal News, 156; s. c., 4 Cent. L. J. 237; s. c., 15 Alb. L. J. 121.

A suit in a State court, *to restrain or stay execution of a judgment of the State court* by a seizure and sale of the complainant's lands, may be removed, under the act of 1875, although such an injunction has been allowed by the State court, if the requisites as to citizenship and amount exist, notwithstanding the Federal courts are prohibited by the Revised Statutes (sec. 720) from granting an injunction to stay proceedings in a State court; and the Federal court has power, under the act of March 3, 1875 (sec. 4), to continue, modify or dissolve the injunction allowed by the State court. Watson v. Bondurant, 2 Woods C. C. 166 (1875). Woods, Circuit Judge; s. c., 3 Cent. L. J. 398.

Right of removal, under act of 1875, of a *railway foreclosure suit* held not affected by the *pendency of another suit* in the State court by stockholders against the company, in which certain orders had been made as to a *receiver;* the right of removal was sustained. Scott *et al.,* Trustees,

name of the real party in interest (as authorized by the State codes), instead of the person holding the bare legal title.[30]

Where the suit in the State court is in its nature a *suit in equity*, it must proceed as an equity cause on its removal into the Federal court. The pleadings and practice in law actions, except where otherwise specially provided by act

v. Clinton & Springfield R. R. Co.."(Drummond, J.), 8 Ch. Legal News 210; s. c., 6 Bissell. 529.

As to the removal of *torts* by one defendant under act of 1866. *quære* in Vannevar v. Bryant, 21 Wall. 41. 43; s. c. below. Bryant v. Rich, 106 Mass. 180. An action of *tort* against several defendants, for a *conspiracy*, can not be removed by part of them under the act of 1866, the Court being of opinion that there could not be a final determination of the *controversy* without the presence of all of the defendants. *Ex parte* Andrews and Mott, 40 Ala. 639 (1867)—Byrd, J., dissenting. The opinion discusses quite fully the construction of the acts of 1866 and 1867. The suit was brought in Alabama by citizens of the state against a citizen of that state and two citizens of another state; and it was held that the act of 1867 did not authorize its removal at the instance of the nonresident defendants. *Ib.*

Definition of "suit," "action," "case," "cases in law and equity." see Story Com. on Const., secs. 1645. 1647. Weston v. City of Charleston. 2 Pet. 449; Holmes v. Jennison. 14 Pet. 540; *Ex parte* Milligan, 4 Wall. 2; Phillips' Pr. (2d Ed.) 13, 55; West v. Aurora. 6 Wall. 139.

What is a suit or defense *arising under a law* of the United States, Turton v. Union Pacific R. R. Co.. 3 Dillon, 366; Orner v. Saunders. *Ib.* 284; People v. Chicago & Alton R. R. Co., (construction of act of Congress of April 20, 1871). 6 Ch. Legal News.316; Osborn v. Bank of U. S., 9 Wheat. 738. Other cases cited *ante*, sec. 8.

Acts of 1866—Removal by part of defendants. The grantor in a deed of trust conveying the legal title in fee to a trustee to secure the payment of a debt to a third person can not under the act of 1866 remove a suit to foreclose such deed of trust in which he and the said trustee are defendants. leaving the trustee in the State court; and the reason is that the foreclosure by sale of land requires the presence of the party holding the legal title; and since. under the act of 1866, the cause was not removable as to the trustee. it could not be removed by the mortgagor. Gardner v. Brown. U. S. Sup. Court. Oct. Term. 1874, 21 Wall. 36; Coal Co. v. Blatchford. 11 Wall. 172; *supra*, sec. 6; *infra*. sec. 13.

[30]Thompson v. Railroad Companies, 6 Wall. 134; Weed Sewing Machine Co. v. Wicks *et al.*, 3 Dillon, 261; Bushnell v. Kennedy. 9 Wall. 391; Act June 1, 1872, 17 Stats. at Large, 197, sec. 5; Rev. Stats., sec. 914; Wood. v. Davis. 18 How. 467; Knapp v. Railroad Co.. 20 Wall. 117. Compare Suydam v. Ewing, 2 Blatchf. 359. as to which *quære*.

of Congress, are to be conformed, as nearly as may be, to the pleadings and practice in the State court of the particular state. But in equity it is otherwise. The pleadings and practice in equity causes in the Federal courts are uniform throughout the United States, and are governed by the Equity Rules prescribed by the Supreme Court of the United States and by the practice of the Court of Chancery in Great Britain as it existed before the recent changes in the judicial system of that country. The Federal courts have the same chancery jurisdiction in every state, and equity causes must be kept separate and distinct, from their inception to the end, from law actions, and are to be decided by principles of equity of uniform and general application.[51]

Where the suit in the State court *unites legal and equitable grounds of relief or of defense* as authorized by the codes, and it is removed, as it may be if the causes for removal exist, what is to be done with it in the Federal court, where law and equity suits and issues must be kept separate and distinct? In such a case *a repleader is necessary*, and the case must be cast in a legal mold, or in the equity mold, or be recast into two cases, one at law and one in equity, and the Federal court is undoubtedly competent to make all orders necessary to this end.[52]

---

51 Neves v. Scott, 13 How. 268. See also Green v. Custard, 23 How. 484, where the reader will find, and perhaps be amused by, the Philippic of Mr. Justice Grier against the code system of pleadings and practice. His remarks are unjust to that system properly understood, but they are too often deserved by the loose practice which has grown up under it.

52 Sands v. Smith, 1 Dillon, 290, note; Fisk v. Union Pacific R. R. Co., 8 Blatchf. 299; Partridge v. Ins. Co. (set-off), 15 Wall. 573.

The text states the practice which has been pursued in the 8th Circuit; and the case of Akerly v. Vilas, 3 Bissell. 332, is not to be understood, we think, as authorizing legal and equitable grounds of relief or defense to be tried in one and the same suit after the removal to the Federal court, nor necessarily to confine the Federal court to the trial of the issues as made up on the pleadings in the State court. The practice in the Federal courts is quite general to allow amendments after the removal, in furtherance of justice and within the scope of the original cause of complaint. Toucey v. Bowen, 1 Bissell, 81 (1855). Huntington, J.; Suydam v. Ewing (practice after removal), 2 Blatchf. 359 (1852).

In *law cases,* pure and simple, *no repleader* in the Federal
courts is necessary, especially since the Practice Act of June
1, 1872.[3] Nor is a repleader necessary *in equity causes*
where the complaint or petition in the State court contains
the substance of a bill in equity adapted to present the
plaintiff's case. But although a repleader in such case be
not indispensable, it may often be advisable. In cases,
however, where legal and equitable matters are united or
mingled, it is necessary, as above stated, to frame the
pleadings anew after the cause reaches the Federal court,

Betts, J.; Barclay v. Levee Commissioners, 1 Woods C. C., 254; Dart v.
McKinney, 9 Blatchf. 359 (1872).
[3] Rev. Stats. sec. 914; Merchants' etc. Nat. Bank v. Wheeler (South.
Dist. N. Y.; Johnson, Circuit J.), 3 Cent. L. J. 13 (1875); Dart v. Mc-
Kinney, 9 Blatchf. 359 (1872), Blatchford, J., under act of 1866. Formerly in cases removed under the Judiciary Act, and where the pleadings
in the Federal court were different from those in the State courts, the
practice in some of the courts was to require the plaintiff after the removal to file a *new declaration,* the same as if the suit had originally been
commenced in the Federal court. Martin v. Kanouse, 1 Blatchf. C. C.
149; s. c., 15 How. 198.

Under the Revised Statutes, sec. 639, the party removing the cause
is required to file in the Federal court " copies of the said process against
him and of all pleadings, depositions, testimony or other proceedings in
the cause," and " when the said copies are entered as aforesaid in the Circuit court, the cause shall there proceed in the same manner, as if it had
been brought there by original process, and the *copies* of pleadings shall
have the same force and effect, *in every respect and for every purpose,* as
the original pleadings would have had by the laws and practice of the
courts of such state, if the cause had remained in the State court." This
clearly dispenses with the necessity of new pleadings in the Federal
court, where the original pleadings are adapted to the separate law and
equity jurisdiction of that court,—the obvious purpose of this legislation
being that the Federal court shall take up the cause where it was when
it left the State court, and proceed with it as if it had been originally
brought in the Federal court. And, in substance, the same provisions
are made in the act of March 3, 1875. See secs. 3, 4, 6, 7.

Costs in suits removed from the State court held to be governed, not by
the Revised Statutes, sec. 968, but by the statute of the state; hence
where, in an action of trespass on the case removed from the State court,
the plaintiff recovered less than $100, it was held that under the statute
of Michigan (Comp. Laws. sec. 7290) the defendant was entitled to costs
as a matter of right. Scupps v. Campbell (East. Dist. Mich., Brown, J),
3 Cent. L. J. 521 (1876).

so as to make it distinctively one at law or one in equity, or by a division into two, the one a law, the other an equity suit.[54]

SECTION X.

FROM WHAT COURT THE REMOVAL MAY BE MADE—REMOVAL HOW ENFORCED—CERTIORARI.

The language of the Revised Statutes, sec. 639, and of the act of March 3, 1875, is: "Any suit in *any* State court," etc. In Gaines v. Fuentes the Supreme Court of the United States held that an action in form and purpose to annul a will and to recall the decree by which it was pro bated, brought in a State court without separate equity jurisdiction, and which is invested with jurisdiction over the estates of deceased persons, might be removed under the act of 1867 to the Federal court. Speaking of the case before the court and the act of 1867, Mr. Justice Field observed: "This act covered every possible case involving controversies between citizens of the state where the suit was brought and citizens of other states, if the matter in dispute, exclusive of costs, exceeded the sum of $500. *It mattered not whether the suit was brought in a State court of limited or general jurisdiction.* The only test was, did it involve a controversy between citizens of the state and citizens of other states, and did the amount in dispute exceed a specified amount? And a controversy was involved in the sense of the statute whenever any property or claim of the parties, capable of pecuniary estimation, was the subject of litigation, and was presented by the pleadings for judicial determination."[55]

---

[54] See Dart v. McKinney. 9 Blatchf. 359; Akerly v. Vilas. 2 Bissell. 110; Green v. Custard. 23 How. 484; Fisk v. Union Pacific R. R. Co.. 8 Blatchf. 299; Partridge v. Ins. Co.. 15 Wall. 573; Sands v. Smith. 1 Dillon. 290; Thompson v. Railroad Cos.. 6 Wall. 134; Rev. Stats.. secs. 639, 914.

[55] Gaines v. Fuentes *et al..* 3 Cent. L. J. 371; s. c.. 8 Ch. Legal News, 225; s. c., 2 Otto. 10. In The Rathbone Oil Co. v. Rauch. 5 West Va.

Under the act of March 3, 1875 (sec. 7), the Circuit
court of the United States, to which any cause shall be removable, under its provisions has power to issue a writ of
certiorari to the State court, commanding that court to make
return of the record in the cause ; and the clerk of the State
court is subjected to criminal punishment who refuses, after
tender of fees, to the party applying for the removal a copy
of the record.[56]

79 (1871). referred to *infra*, it was held that no motion to remove a cause
can be made before a justice of the peace. that not being a " State court "
within the meaning of the act of Congress.—but the act of Congress is,
" *any* State court." whether of general or limited jurisdiction.

[56] *Certiorari — Copies of record—Mandamus to enforce removal, etc*.—
The only object of a *certiorari* is to bring the record from the State court
into the Federal court; but the writ is unnecessary, when the record of
the State court is already before the Federal court. Scott *et al.*, Trustees,
v. Clinton and Springfield R. R. Co., 8 Ch. Legal News. 210, *per* Drummond. J.: s. c., 6 Bissell, 529.

The writ of *certiorari* is often resorted to as the means of effecting,
pursuant to law, the removal of the record of a proceeding or cause from
one court to another. In England and in some of the states in this
country indictments and other proceedings are removed for trial from
the lower to the higher court. Bacon's Abridg. title *Certiorari*; 1 Bl.
Com. 320. 321: 1 Chitty Cr. Law, 334, 571 *et seq.*, 387; State v. Gibbons.
1 South. (N. J.), 40. 44; United States v. McKee, 4 Dillon, C. C. (not yet
reported); s. c., 3 Cent. L. J. 292, on motion in arrest of judgment.

Section 7 of the act of March 3, 1875. authorizing the Circuit court to
issue the writ of *certiorari*. provides that it shall " command the State
court to make return of the record " of the cause removed, which means
an exemplified copy of the record. United States v. McKee. *supra*. And
express power is given to the Circuit court " to enforce the said writ according to law."

The provision in the act of March 3, 1875. sec. 7, in respect to *certiorari*.
only extends to " causes which shall be removable under *this act*." There
is no similar provision as to cases removable under sec. 639 of the Revised Statutes; but there is a provision (Rev. Stats. sec. 645) allowing
copies of the record in the State court to be supplied by affidavit or otherwise. on proof that the clerk of the State court. after demand and payment or tender of his legal fees. refuses or neglects to deliver certified
copies of the records and proceedings of the State court in the cause. As
to provisions in special cases, see Revised Statutes. secs. 641. 643; Benchley v. Gilbert (suit held not removable by *certiorari* under sec. 67. act of
July 13, 1866), 8 Blatchf. 147.

Certiorari and habeas corpus under act of 1833. " force act." in respect
to removal of causes. Abranches v. Schell. 4 Blatchf. 256.

SECTION XI.

AS TO VALUE.

In the REMOVAL acts to which we have referred, namely, the Revised Statutes, section 639, and the act of March 3, 1875, it is made an indispensable element of removability, that the *amount in dispute*, exclusive of costs, shall " exceed the sum or value of five hundred dollars." This language, as well as that which precedes it, is descriptive of the nature of *suits* that may be removed. The subject-matter of the dispute or of the suit must be property, or money, or some right, the value of which in money is susceptible of judicial ascertainment. The language descriptive of *suits that may be removed* excludes criminal cases and controversies relating to the custody of a child, or the right to personal freedom.[57]

As to *order allowing copies* of the papers, etc.. in the State court to be filed in the Federal court, where the clerk refuses to certify such copies: Akerly v. Vilas. 1 Abb. U. S. Rep. 284; s. c., 2 Bissell. 110 (1869); 24 Wis. 165; Hatch v. C., R. I. & P. R. R. Co., 6 Blatchf. 105.

Without express authority from Congress, the Federal court can not issue a writ of *mandamus* to the State court, to require it to proceed no further in the case, and to certify the case to the Federal court. It was admitted that Congress could confer such a power, but denied that it had done so by the Judiciary Act. *Per* Drummond, J.. Hough v. West. Transp. Co.. 1 Bissell, 425 (1864). Or by the act of July 27. 1866; *In re* Cromie, 2 Bissell. 160 (1869). Or by the act of July 27,1868 (Rev. Stats.. sec. 640): Fisk v. Union Pacific B. R. Co.. 6 Blatchf. 362 (1869). See on subject of *mandamus* and process to enforce removal of cause from State to Federal court, Spraggins v. County Court, Cooke's Rep. 160. *Ex parte* Turner. 3 Wall. Jr. 258. Grier, J.

Proceedings in the State court after the removal of the cause will not be stayed by writ from the Federal court: if the removal was not lawfully effected, such writ is improper: if effected. it is unnecessary. Bell v. Dix, 49 N. Y. 232 (1872): Fisk v. Union Pacific R. R. Co.. 6 Blatchf. 362. See further on this point, *post.* sec. 17 and note.

[57] Phillips' Pr. (2d Ed.). 82: Lee v. Lee. 8 Pet. 44; Barry v. Mercien. 5 How. 103; Pratt v. Fitzhugh, 1 Black, 271: DeKrafft v. Barney, 2 Black. 704; Sparrow v. Strong. 3 Wall. 97: Gaines v. Fuentes. Sup. Court, Oct. Term. 1875. 3 Cent. L. J. 371: s. c.. 2 Otto. 10. The suits must relate to claims or property capable of pecuniary estimation. *Ib.*

It is not sufficient that the value in dispute *precisely equals* $500 ; it must *exceed* that sum or amount.[58]

The value of the matter in dispute for the purposes of removal is to be determined by reference to the amount claimed in the declaration, petition or bill of complaint.[59] In actions on a *money demand*, the value in dispute is the debt and damages claimed as stated in the petition or declaration, and in the prayer for judgment. For example, if the action be on a note for a fixed sum, and the principal and interest and damages do not all together exceed $500, it is not removable, although the prayer for judgment may be for an amount greater than $500. On the other hand, in the case supposed, though the plaintiff might have been entitled to a recovery for more than $500, yet if the prayer for judgment be for *less* than that amount, the case could not be removed.[60]

It is sufficient that the amount in dispute exceeds $500 *at the time* when the right to a removal accrues and is applied for—and *interest*, when the right thereto exists and it is claimed, may be regarded in determining the amount or value in controversy.[61] The State court decisions, proceeding on a different principle, are probably unsound.

In actions *sounding in tort* the damages laid by the plaintiff are the amount of the matter in dispute.[62]

---

[58] Walker v. United States, 4 Wall. 163; W. U. Tel. Co. v. Levi, 47 Ind. 552.

[59] Gordon v. Longest. 16 Pet. 97; Kanouse v. Martin, 15 How. 198. 207; Ladd v. Tudor, 3 Woodb. & Minot, 325; Muns v. Dupont, 2 Wash. C. C. 463: Bennett v. Butterworth (detinue), 8 How. 124; Peyton v. Robertson (replevin). 9 Wheat. 527; United States v. McDowell (penal bonds). 4 Cranch. 316: Martin v. Taylor (penalty). 1 Wash. C. C. 1; Postmaster-General v. Cross (penal bond). 4 Wash. C. C. 326; King v. Wilson (illegal taxes). 1 Dillon, 555: Hartshorn v. Wright (ejectment). 1 Pet. C. C. 64; Crawford v. Burnham (ejectment), 4 Am. Law Times, 228; W. U. Tel. Co. v. Levi, 47 Ind. 552.

[60] See Lee v. Watson. 1 Wall. 337.

[61] McGinnity v. White. 3 Dillon. 350; Bank etc. v. Daniel. 12 Pet. 32; Merrill v. Petty, 16 Wall. 338.

[62] Hulsecamp v. Teel. 2 Dallas, 358; Gordon v. Longest. 16 Pet. 97; West. Union Tel. Co. v. Levi. 47 Ind. 552.

Where the right to a removal has become perfect and complete, it is not in the power of the other party to defeat it in either court by release or by amendment of petition and declaring for less than five hundred dollars.[63]

It is made a condition of the right to an appeal or writ of error to the Supreme Court that the " matter in dispute exceeds the sum or value of two (now five) thousand dollars, exclusive of costs." The cases arising under this clause are collected and accurately stated by Mr. Phillips,[64] and will be found, in many instances, applicable to questions arising in this regard under the removal acts.

In leaving this point, we may be permitted to observe that in our judgment the most serious objection to the removal acts, as they now exist, is the small amount required to authorize a removal. In view of the inconvenience and expense of litigating in the Federal courts, held often more than one hundred miles distant from the residence of the parties ; the crowded state of their dockets : and considering that removals, especially by foreign insurance and railway corporations, often have the effect to delay, if not to oppress, those having claims against them, it is quite clear that the amount to justify a removal should be enlarged, or the Federal courts multiplied, or at all events their judicial force increased.

SECTION XII.

PARTY ENTITLED TO A REMOVAL.—CITIZENSHIP— CORPORATIONS—ALIENS.

Under the 12th section of the Judiciary Act, omitting the case of aliens, the right of removal is limited, as we have shown, to the non-resident defendant, when sued by a resident plaintiff. Under the act of 1866 it is limited. as we have seen, under the restrictions therein imposed, to the non-

---

[63] Kanouse v. Martin. 15 How. 198; Wright v. Wells, 1 Pet. C. C. 220: Green v. Custard, 23 How. 468: Roberts v. Nelson. 8 Blatchf. 74.

[64] Practice of the Supreme Court. chap. VIII.

resident defendant, and it is not given either to the resident defendant or to the resident plaintiff. Under the act
of 1867 the right is given, as above shown, under the
enumerated conditions, to the plaintiff *or* defendant ; but in
either case it is only the non-resident citizen who can remove the case.[65]

Where the jurisdiction of the Federal court depends on
citizenship, it is the citizenship of the parties to the record
that is alone considered, and not of those who, although
not parties, may be beneficially interested in the litigation.
This rule applies to executors and administrators and
trustees.[66]

[65] Citizenship of a state, for the purpose of conferring Federal jurisdiction, has reference to domicile and residence, not the right of suffrage.
D'Wolf v. Raband. 1 Pet. 476; s. c.. Paine C. C. 580; Case v. Clarke 5
Mason C. C. 70: Cooper v. Galbraith. 3 Wash. C. C. 546: Shelton v. Tiflin.
6 How. 163: Lanz v. Randall (Dist. Minn.. Miller, J). 3 Cent. L. J. 688
(1876). Effect of *bona fide change of domicile*. Jones v. League, 18 How.
76: Morgan's Heirs v. Morgan. 2 Wheat. 290; United States v. Myers.
2 Brock. 516.

A *State* can not make the *subject of a foreign government* a citizen of
the United States: and *resident unnaturalized foreigners* may remove
causes to the Federal court on the ground that they are aliens, although
by state laws they may vote at elections or hold office under the state
government. Lanz v. Randall (Dist. Minn.. Mr. Justice Miller), 3 Cent.
L. J. 688 (1876) ; *ante*, sec. 6. *note*.

[66] If the *administrator or executor* and the defendant are citizens of the
same state, the Federal court has no jurisdiction. although the intestate
or testator was a citizen of a different state. Coal Co. v. Blatchford. 11
Wall. 172: Dodge v. Perkins. 4 Mason C. C. 435; Childress v. Emory. 8
Wheat. 642; Carter v. Treadwell. 3 Story C. C. 25; Green's Adminis-
tratrix v. Creighton. 23 How. 90. If the action is by or against the deceased. the executor or administrator may prosecute or defend it without
reference to his own citizenship. Clarke v. Mathewson. 12 Pet. 164;
s. c. below. 2 Sumner C. C. 262. *The citizenship of executors* is determined
by the state of which they are citizens; and the circumstance that they
have taken out letters in another state does not make them citizens of
such state. Amory v. Amory. 36 N. Y. Superior Court Rep. (4 Jones &
Spencer). 520 (1874) : Geyer v. Life Ins. Co.. 50 N. H. 224 (1870). If he
remove to another state and become. in respect of jurisdiction. a citizen
thereof. he may sue in the Circuit court of the State in which his letters
were granted. Rice v. Houston. 13 Wall. 66.

Citizenship of trustees. Bonnafee v. Williams. 3 How. 574; Coal Co. v.
Blatchford. 11 Wall. 172; Gardner v. Brown. 21 Wall. 36: Thompson v..

Corporations created by the states are within all the removal acts under consideration, and after much uncertainty and fluctuation of opinion in the Supreme Court of the United States, the settled rule now is that a corporation, for all purposes of Federal jurisdiction, is conclusively considered as if it were a citizen of the state which created it, and no averment or proof as to citizenship of its members elsewhere is competent or material.[67]

The same principle applies to *public and municipal corporations*—they are for jurisdictional purposes necessarily

Railroad Companies, 6 Wall. 134; Weed Sewing Machine Co. v. Wicks *et al.*, 3 Dillon, 261; Bushnell v. Kennedy, 9 Wall. 391; Act June 1, 1872, 17 Stats. at Large, 197, sec. 5; Rev. Stats., sec. 914; Wood v. Davis, 18 How. 467; Knapp v. Railroad Co., 20 Wall. 117. Compare Suydam v. Ewing, 2 Blatchf. 359, as to which *quære*.

Who are to be regarded as parties to a bill in equity filed by the complainant in behalf of himself and *such others as might come in and become parties*, see Hazard v. Durant, 9 R. I. 602 (1868).

[67] Railroad Co. v. Harris, 12 Wall. 65, 81; Railway Co. v. Whitton, 13 Wall. 270, 285; Louisville etc. R. R. Co. v. Letson, 2 How. 497; Marshall v. The Baltimore & Ohio Railroad Co., 16 How. 314; The Covington Drawbridge Company v. Shepherd *et al.* 20 How. 232; Ohio & Mississippi Railroad Company v. Wheeler. 1 Black, 286; Trust Co. v. Macnillan (act of 1867) 3 Dillon, 379; Minnett v. Milwaukee & St. Paul Railway Co. (act of 1867), 3 Dillon, 460. As to the effect on Federal jurisdiction (where it is dependent upon the citizenship of the parties) of *charters granted by different states to the same company* or to companies constructing the same line of road, and as to the *effect of consolidation* on the jurisdiction of the Federal courts, the following are the principal cases: Ohio & Miss. R. R. Co. v. Wheeler. 1 Black, 286; Balt. & Ohio R. R. Co. v. Harris, 12 Wall. 65; Ch. & N. W. R. R. Co. v. Whitton, 13 Wall. 270; Williams v. M. K. & T. Railway Co., 3 Dillon, 267. See also, Marshall v. B. & O. R. R. Co., 16 How. 314; Balt. & O. R. R. Co. v. Gallahue's Administrator, 12 Grattan, 658; Goshorn v. Supervisors, 1 West. Va. 308; Minot v. Phila. Wil. & B. R. R. Co., 2 Abb. U. S. R. 323. See Chicago & Northwestern Railroad Company v. Chicago & Pacific Railroad Company, 8 Chicago Legal News (Nov. 14, 1874), 57, (s. c. 6 Bissell, 219), decided by Circuit Judge Drummond, as to the effect of consolidation under charters of different states and the citizenship of the consolidated company.

What is a sufficient statement and averment of the *citizenship of corporations to sustain Federal jurisdiction*: Express Co. v. Kountze, 8 Wall. 342; Ins. Co. v. Francis, 11 Wall. 210; Manuf. Bank v. Baack, 8 Blatchf. 137; s. c., 2 Abb. U. S. Rep. 232; Covington Drawbridge Co. v. Shep-

4

citizens of the state under whose laws they are created and organized.[68]

A *corporation of another state* may remove a cause commenced by attachment of property, although the action could not, by reason of a citizenship in a legal sense out of the district, and inability to serve it within the district, be commenced by original process in the Circuit court of the United States ;[69] and the right to a removal in such a case is not lost by reason of such corporation having an office for the transaction of business in the state in which the suit is

herd, 20 How. 227; Piquignot v. Pa. R. R. Co.. 16 How. 104; Ohio. & Miss. R. R. Co. v. Wheeler. 1 Black. 286.

As to the right of *joint stock companies, partly but not fully endowed with the attributes of corporations.* to sue in the Federal court, or remove cases to the Federal court on the ground of citizenship or alienage, there is some diversity of judicial decision. The leading cases on this point are : Liverpool Ins. Co. v. Massachusetts, 10 Wall. 566; Penn. v. Quicksilver Mining Co.. 10 Wall. 553; Dinsmore v. Phila. etc. R. R. Co. (McKennan. Circuit Judge). 3 Cent. L. J. 157; Maltz v. Am. Express Co. (Brown, J.). 3 Cent. L. J. 784.

[68] Cowles v. Mercer County, 7 Wall. 118; Barclay v. Levee Commrs. 1 Woods C. C. 254. In McCoy v. Washington County, 3 Wall. Jr. C. C. 381, it was contended " that the County of Washington, merely a subordinate political division of the State of Pennsylvania, is not a citizen of this state, within the meaning of the Constitution or the act of Congress, and therefore not suable in this court." " To this we answer," says Grier. J., " that though the metaphysical entity called a corporation may not be physically a citizen. yet the law is well settled, that it may sue and be sued in the courts of the United States. because it is but the name under which a number of persons. corporators and citizens may sue and be sued. In deciding the question of jurisdiction. the court look behind the name, to find who are the parties really in interest. In this case the parties to be affected by the judgment are the people of Washington County. That the defendant is a municipal corporation and not a private one, furnishes a stronger reason why a citizen of another state should have his remedy in this court, and not in a county where the parties. against whom the remedy is sought, would compose the court and jury to decide their own case. This point is therefore overruled." A state statute can not limit the liability of a municipal corporation to be sued in the courts of a state. so as to affect the Federal jurisdiction. Cowles v. Mercer County. 7 Wall. 118; Railway Co. v. Whitton, 13 Wall. 270.

[69] Bliven v. New. Eng. Screw Co., 3 Blatchf. 111; Barney v. Globe Bank. 5 ib. 107; Sayles v. N. W. Ins. Co.. 2 Curtis, 212.

brought.[70] Nor can such a corporation be deprived of the right of removal by state legislation.[71]

Incorporated bodies chartered by foreign countries may remove cases under the provisions as to *aliens*.[72]

For jurisdictional purposes *national banks* are deemed citizens of the state in which they are located,[73] and they may sue in the Circuit court, although the defendants are citizens of the same state in which the bank is established.[74] The act of July 27, 1868 (Revised Statutes, sec. 640, *ante*, sec. 2, note), expressly excludes national banks from its provisions : but this has been considered not to prevent the right of removal in their favor, if their case is within any of the other removal acts.[75]

[70] Hatch v. Chicago etc. R. R. Co., 6 Blatchf. 105. The right of a foreign corporation to remove a cause is not affected by the legislature of the state authorizing *service of process on its agent* in the state. W. U. Tel. Co. v. Dickinson, 40 Ind. 444 (1872); Hobbs v. Manhattan Ins. Co., 56 Maine, 417; Morton v. Mut. Life Ins. Co., 105 Mass. 141 (1870). A foreign corporation, sued by its own assent in another state, is notwithstanding a foreign corporation, and for all purposes of Federal jurisdiction a citizen of the state which created it. Pomeroy v. N. Y. & N. H. R. R. Co., 5 Blatchf. C. C. 120; Hatch v. Ch., R. I. & P. R. R. Co., 6 Blatchf. 105.

[71] Chicago etc. Railway Co. v. Whitton's Admrs., 13 Wall. 270; *ante*, sec. 3 and cases cited.

[72] Terry v. Ins. Co., 3 Dillon, 408; 1 Kent's Com. 348; see also Angell & Ames on Corporations, secs. 377, 378, and 1 Abbott's U. S. Practice, 216; Fisk v. Ch. etc. Railroad Co., 53 Barb. 472; 3 Abb. Pr. Rep. (N. S.) 453; King of Spain v. Oliver 2 Washington C. C. 429.

[73] Chatham Nat. Bank v. Mer. Nat. Bank, 1 Hun, (N. Y.), 702. See, also, to the effect that for jurisdictional purposes national banks are citizens of the state where they are located: Davis v. Cook, 9 Nev. 134 (1874), following Manuf. Nat. Bank v. Baack, 2 Abb. U. S. Rep. 232; s. c., 8 Blatchf. 137, and approving of the reasoning of Blatchford, J. Same point, Cook v. State National Bank, 52 N. Y. 96 (1873); s. c. below, 50 Barb. 339, 1 Lans. 494, holding that national banks are citizens of the state in which they are located, and may apply as such for the removal of causes.

[74] Union Nat. Bank v. Chicago, 3 Ch. Legal News, 369; Bank of Omaha v. Douglas County, 3 Dillon C. C. 298; Com. Bank v. Simmons, 6 Ch. Legal News, 344.

[75] In the Chatham Nat. Bank of New York v. Mer. Nat. Bank of West. Va., 1 Hun (N. Y.), 702, a national bank was regarded as a citizen of the

But there is a distinction between National Banking Associations and the *Receivers* of such associations ; neither under the Revised Statutes (sec. 640), nor under the National Banking Act (sec. 57), have such receivers as such the right to remove cases from the State courts into the Federal courts.[76]

SECTION XIII.

THE TIME WHEN THE APPLICATION MUST BE MADE.

Under the 12th section of the Judiciary Act (now Revised Statutes, sec. 639, sub-division 1), the application must be made by the defendant " at the *time* of *entering his appearance* in the State court." Under this provision the defendant must promptly avail himself of this right, and he waives it if he demurs, or pleads, or answers, or otherwise submits himself to the jurisdiction of the State court.[77]

state in which it is located and does business, and the national bank of another state may remove a suit in which it is a defendant, if the case is otherwise within the 12th section of the Judiciary Act, and the application is made in time, *i. e.*, at the time of " entering its appearance;" and this, notwithstanding the act of July 27. 1868 (15 Stats. at Large, 226; Rev. Stats.. sec. 640), excludes national banking associations from its provisions—the latter being considered as providing for a new class of cases, and not affecting the right of removal given by preceding legislation.

[76] Bird's Executors v. Cockrem, Receiver. 2 Woods C. C. 32. Bradley, J.

[77] West v. Aurora City. 6 Wall. 139; Sweeney v. Coffin. 1 Dillon, 73; Webster v. Crothers, 1 Dillon. 301; Johnson v. Monell. 1 Woolw. 390; McBratney v. Usher. 1 Dillon. 367. 369; Robinson v. Potter (too late after reference and continuance). 43 N. H. 188; Savings Bank v. Benton, 2 Metc. (Ky.) 240; *supra*. sec. 5, and cases cited.

As to the right of *different* defendants to remove at *different times*, see Smith v. Rines. 2 Sumn. 338; Ward v. Arredondo. 1 Paine, 410; Beardsley v. Torrey. 4 Wash. C. C. 286; Field v. Lownsdale, 1 Deady. 288; Fisk v. Union Pacific R. R. Co.. 8 Blatchf. 243. 299; *supra*, sec. 5. and cases cited.

The State court can not restore right of removal by allowing an ap-

Under the acts of 1866 and 1867 (now Revised Statutes, sec. 639, sub-divisions 2 and 3), the time is enlarged, and the petition for the removal may be made " at *any time before* the trial or final hearing of the suit " in the State court. The word "trial " refers to cases at law—" hearing," to suits in equity.[78] Under this language the petition for the removal *may*, it is certain, be made at any time before entering upon the final trial, or the hearing on the merits ; and it *must* be made before *final judgment in the court of original jurisdiction*, and it is too late to make it after the cause has reached, and is pending in the State appellate court.[79]

" Before final hearing or trial clearly means," says Mr.

pearance to be entered *nunc pro tunc.* Ward v. Arredondo, 1 Paine, 410; Gibson v. Johnson, Pet. C. C. 44.

[78] Vannevar v. Bryant, 21 Wall. 41, 43, *per* Waite, C. J.; s. c. below, Bryant v. Rich, 106 Mass. 180.

[79] Stevenson v. Williams, 19 Wall. 572; Vannevar v. Bryant, 21 Wall. 41, 43; Waggener v. Cheek, 2 Dillon, 560; Kellogg v. Hughes, 3 Dillon, 357; Dart v. McKinney, 9 Blatchf. 359; Johnson v. Monell (change of residence pending suit), 1 Woolw. 390; Minnett v. Milwaukee & St. Paul Railway Co., 3 Dillon, 460, denying Galpin v. Critchlow, 13 Am. Law Reg. (N. S.), 137; s. c., 112 Mass. 339, and Whittier v. Hartford Ins. Co., 14 Am. Law Reg. (N. S.), 121; s. c. 55 N. H. 141; see Ins. Co. v. Dunn, 19 Wall. 214, 225; Akerly v. Vilas, 1 Abb. U. S. Rep. 284; s. c. 2 Bissell, 110; Murray v. Justices, 9 Wall. 274; Miller v. Finn, 1 Neb. 254 (1867); Price v. Sommers (N. D. Ohio, Welker, J.), 8 Ch. Legal News, 290 (1876); Fasnacht v. Frank (U. S. Sup. Court, Oct. 1874), 23 Wall. 416; Craigie v. McArthur, 9 Ch. Legal News, 156.

What was a "final trial " within the meaning of the act of 1867 (Rev. Stats., sec. 639, cl. 3), was considered in West Virginia in a case of unlawful detainer, commenced before a justice of the peace, where judgment went against a citizen of another state, who appealed to the Circuit court, and then applied to remove the case to the Federal court under the act of 1867. The lower court denied the application, and rendered judgment against the defendant, and on appeal the Court of Appeals reversed the judgment, resting its decision upon two grounds : 1. No motion to remove could have been made before the justice, that not being a "State court " within the meaning of the act of Congress. 2. The case on appeal from a justice is to be tried *de novo* in the Circuit court the same as if never tried, and hence there was no "final trial " within the intent of the act of Congress. Rathbone Oil Co. v. Rauch, 5 West Va. 79 (1871).

Justice Field, " before final judgment in the court of original jurisdiction, where the suit is brought. Whether it
may not mean still more—before the hearing or trial of the
suit has commenced, which is followed by such judgment
—may be questioned; but it is unnecessary to determine
that question in this case."[80] It would seem, however, that
it would be too late to defer the application, until the trial
was actually entered on.[81]

Although there is some conflict between the State and
Federal courts on the point, yet the weight of the cases and
the authoritative view is, that if the trial court has wholly
set aside a verdict and granted a new trial, or if the State
appellate court has *wholly reversed the judgment* and remanded the case to the court of original jurisdiction for a
trial *de novo*, then, in either event, it is not too late under
the act of 1866 or 1867, to apply to remove the cause, as it
is in the same posture as before the first trial or hearing
was had.[82]

[80] Stevenson v. Williams, *supra*; Beery v. Irick, 22 Gratt. (Va.), 487
(1872); Williams v. Williams, 24 La. Ann. 55; Douglas v. Caldwell.
(" final hearing" what?) 65 N. C. 248 (1871).

[81] Application for removal, under the acts of 1866 and 1867, must
be made *before trial or hearing commences*; it is too late if made during
the progress of the trial, and this principle is not varied by the fact, that
during the trial an amendment of the declaration was allowed on which
issue was not joined at the time the petition to remove the case was filed.
Adams Express Co. v. Trego, 35 Md. 47 (1871); see also Lewis v. Smythe
(Woods, Circuit Judge), 2 Woods C. C. 117 (1875), referred to *infra*.

[82] Vannevar v. Bryant. 21 Wall. 41, 43, *per* Waite, C. J.; s. c., 106
Mass. 180; Stevenson v. Williams, 19 Wall. 572; Waggener v. Cheek. 2
Dillon. 560; Kellogg v. Hughes. 3 Dillon, 357; Dart v. McKinney. 9
Blatchf. 359; Johnson v. Monell (change of residence pending suit). 1
Woolw. 390; Minnett v. Milwaukee & St. Paul Railway Co., 3 Dillon.
460, denying Galpin v. Critchlow, 13 Am. Law Reg. (N. S.) 137; s. c., 112
Mass. 339, and Whittier v. Hartford Ins. Co., 14 Am. Law Reg. (N. S.) 121;
s. c., 55 N. H. 141. See Ins. Co. v. Dunn, 19 Wall. 214. 225; Akerly v.
Vilas, 1 Abb. U. S. Rep. 284; s. c., 2 Bissell, 110; Murray v. Justices, 9
Wall. 274; Fasnacht v. Frank, U. S. Sup. Court. Oct. 1874, *supra;* Dart v.
Walker, 4 Daly (N. Y.). 188 (1871), also holding that under act of 1866
or 1867 removal may be had after a reversal and order for a new trial.

The cases in the State courts holding a different doctrine from that
stated in the text are not sound expositions of the statute. The follow-

The case of the Insurance Co. v. Dunn (19 Wall. 214) affords a striking illustration of the meaning of the phrase, *"final* judgment " in the acts of 1867. The plaintiff in that case had a verdict and judgment thereon in one of the courts of Ohio. The defendant (the Insurance Company) under the statute of the State, applied for a new trial, and gave bond in that behalf. This had the effect, under the statute of the state, *to vacate the verdict and judgment* as if a new trial had been granted, except that *lien of the judg-*ing are some of the more important of these: Hall v. Ricketts, 9 Bush (Ky). 366 (1872); Akerly v. Vilas, 24 Wis. 165; Home Life Ins. Co. v. Dunn, 20 Ohio St. 175; Crane v. Reeder, 28 Mich. 527 (1874); Galpin v. Critchlow, 112 Mass. 339 (1873).

Where the Supreme Court of a State has reversed the decree of the lower court and remanded the cause *with instructions to dismiss the bill,* it is too late to apply for a removal to the Federal court under the act of March 2, 1867. Boggs v. Willard, 3 Bissell, 256 (1872), Blodgett, J. But where the State Supreme Court has ordered a new trial, the plaintiff may dismiss and commence in the Federal court. Hazard v. Chicago etc. R. R. Co., 4 Bissell, 453. Effect of the decision of the State Supreme Court in such a case considered. *Ib.*

The case of McKinley v. Chicago & N. W. Railway Co., now in the Supreme Court of the United States on a writ of error to the Supreme Court of Iowa, presents a new and interesting point. The case in the State court was for personal injury. The plaintiff had a verdict and judgment below. The railway company appealed to the Supreme Court of the State, which reversed the judgment and ordered a new trial, and issued its *procedendo,* which was filed within sixty days in the lower court. Thereupon the railway company in due form made and filed its petition and bond for removal of the cause to the Federal court under the acts of 1867 and 1875. This was in vacation, and there was no order upon it. By the law of the State, causes in the Supreme Court are to be remanded for a new trial, if a new trial be ordered (Code, sec. 3206), and there is a provision for recalling a *procedendo,* if a petition for rehearing be filed in sixty days (Code, sec. 3201). *After* the petition and bond for removal had been filed as above, but *within* the sixty days, a petition for rehearing was filed in the Supreme Court of the State, and the *procedendo* was re-called. The railway company moved the State Supreme Court to dismiss the petition for rehearing, because the court had no further jurisdiction of the cause, inasmuch as the same was duly removed to the Federal court, after the *procedendo* was filed and before it was recalled. The State Supreme Court overruled the motion, and subsequently granted the rehearing and rendered judgment against the railway company, which has sued out a writ of error, which is now pending in the Supreme Court of the United States.

ment remained as security for the plaintiff. When the case
was in this *status*, the company applied to remove the cause
under the act of 1867, and it was held that there had been
no *final* trial, that the application was in time, and that the
suit was removable; and the subsequent judgment in the
State court was reversed by the Supreme Court of the United
States.[83]

But a cause can not be removed where a verdict has been
rendered, and a motion is *pending* to set the verdict aside.
Such a motion must be disposed of, and be granted, so that
the right to a second trial is complete, before the cause can
be transferred, since, says the Chief Justice, " every trial of
a cause is *final* until, in some form, it has been vacated.
Causes can not be removed to the Circuit court for a review
of the action of the State court, but only for trial. The Circuit court can not, after a trial in a State court, determine
whether there shall be another. That is for the State court.

[83] In Ohio, where a case is commenced in the Court of Common Pleas,
where a trial is had, and an appeal taken to the District court of the
State. it is too late, *under the act of* 1875, to apply to remove the case to
the Federal court.   Welker, J., distinguishes this case from Ins. Co.
v. Dunn. 19 Wall. 214. and applies the doctrine of Stevenson v. Williams.
19 Wall. 572. and regards the hearing in the Common Pleas as " final "
within the meaning of the removal act, although the effect of the appeal
is to vacate the decree and entitle the party to a trial *de novo*.   Price v.
Sommers (North. Dist. Ohio), 8 Ch. Legal News. 290 (1876).   Similar
principle in respect to attempt to remove from an appellate court a case
which originated in the Probate court, after a decision and appeal: it
was held not removable.   Craigie v. McArthur (Dist. Minn.. Dillon and
Nelson. JJ.), 9 Ch. Legal News. 156 (1876) ; s. c., 4 Cent. L. J. 237 ; s. c..
15 Alb. L. J. 121.   The plaintiff had a judgment on a verdict ; the defendants sued out a writ of review and then applied. the judgment re-
maining unreversed. to remove the cause under the Revised Statutes. sec.
639. cl. 3 ; *held*. under the legislation of the state as to effect of the
first judgment and of the proceeding for review. and distinguishing the
case from Ins. Co. v. Dunn (19 Wall. 214). that the cause was not removable at that stage.   Whittier v. Hartford Fire Ins. Co.. 55 N. H. 141
(1875). commented on, and its principle applied to a case where the application for removal was made after verdict set aside and a new trial
granted.   Chandler v. Coe. 56 N. H. 184.   *Contra*, Minnett v. Mil. &
St. Paul Railroad Co., 3 Cent. L. J. 281 : s. c.. 3 Dillon. 460, and see cases
cited *ante*.

To authorize the removal, the action must, at the time of the application, be actually pending for trial."[54]

Under the acts of 1866 and 1867, it is sufficient, *it seems*, as respects citizenship, that the defendant applying for the removal is, *at the time* of filing his petition therefor, a citizen of another state, and the plaintiff a citizen of the state in which the suit is brought.[55]

One of several defendants sued as *copartners* may, if the other requisites exist, have the cause removed into the Federal court, so far as concerns himself, under the act of 1866.[56]

Under the act of March 3, 1875 (see. 3), the time for the removal is greater than under the Judiciary Act, but not so great as under the acts of 1866 and 1867 last noticed. The act of 1875 requires the petition in the State court to be made and filed therein " before or at the term at which such cause *could be first tried*, and before the trial thereof." The word term as here used means, according to the construction which it has received in the 8th judicial circuit, the term at which, under the legislation of the state and the rules of practice pursuant thereto, the cause is first triable, *i. e.*, subject to be tried on its merits ; not necessarily the term when, owing to press of business or arrearages, it may be first reached, in its order, for actual trial. This act gives the right of removal to either party—the resident as well as the non-resident party—and no affidavit of prejudice is required : and it was the obvious purpose of Congress by the use of the words " *before* or at, etc., the term at which the cause *could* be *first* tried," etc., to require the election to be taken at the first term at which, under the law, the cause was triable on its merits. The judicial construction elsewhere of the act of 1875 is in accordance with these views.[57]

[54] Vannevar v. Bryant, 21 Wall. 41, 43; s. c., 106 Mass. 180; see Whittier v. Hartford Ins. Co. 55 N. H. 141.

[55] McGinnity v. White, 3 Dillon. 350. *Contra.* Dart v. Walker. 4 Daly (N. Y.). 188 (1871). See *infra.* sec. 14 .

[56] *Ib.;* and see *supra* sec. 6 and sec. 9, note.

[57] Ames v. Colorado Central R. R. Co. (Hallett. J., February. 1877), 4 Cent. L. J. 199.

The decisions under the acts of 1866 and 1867, that a removal may be applied for, after a verdict has been set aside and a new trial granted, or the judgment of the trial court has been wholly reversed and a trial *de novo* awarded, are, it is supposed, inapplicable under the act of 1875, which requires the petition for the removal to be made "*before or at* etc., *the term* at which the cause could be *first tried* and before the trial thereof." It is clearly too late to apply for the removal after a trial has once begun, although it may result in a mistrial, or in a verdict or judgment that may be set aside with an order for a new trial.[88] Accordingly it has

"We understand that Judge Davis, when sitting as circuit justice for the district of Indiana, held that the application for removal must be made at the first term at which the cause could be put at issue, and before the trial thereof." Buskirk's Indiana Practice, 459.

A cause was at issue and could have been tried, but *by consent was continued*. Judge Drummond held, under the act of 1875, that it was too late to remove the case at a subsequent term, as the continuance was neither the act of the law nor of the court. Scott *et al.*, Trustees, v. Clinton & Springfield R. R. Co., 8 Chicago Legal News. 210; s. c., 6 Bissell, 529, where the case thus decided is referred to and distinguished.

A *chancery cause* can not be tried until the issues are made up;—if there is no delay in completing the issues on the part of the applicant for the removal, the application is in time, if made before the lapse of a term at which the cause could have been tried. Whether laches in making up issues will defeat right of removal, if removal be applied for before the issues are completed, *quære?* Scott *et al.*, Trustees. v. Clinton & Springfield R. R. Co., 8 Chicago Legal News, 210; s. c., 6 Bissell. 529, Drummond, J.

Where a replication under the local law and practice is necessary to complete the issue, and where there is no default in making up the issues by the party who applies for a removal of the cause, no term has passed at which the cause could have been tried within the meaning of the act of March 3, 1875, sec. 3. Mich. Central R. R. Co. v. Andes Ins. Co. (S. D. Ohio. Swing. J.), 9 Ch. Legal News, 34. In this case, Swing, J., approves of the construction of the act of 1875, in respect to the time of removals given by Drummond, Circuit Judge, in Scott *et al.*, Trustees, v. Clinton etc. R. R. Co., *supra*.

[88] A party entitled to a removal of a cause, who proceeds to trial without applying for a transfer to the Federal court, is not, under the act of 1875. entitled to a removal at a subsequent term, although a new trial may have been granted him; in this respect the act of 1875 is different from the acts of 1866 and 1867. Young v. Andes Ins. Co. (S. D. Ohio, Swing. J.). 3 Cent. L. J. 719 (1876).

been held, under the act of March 3, 1875, that the application for removal must be made, *before the trial on its merits, or on a question which results in a final judgment or decree,* commences. It is therefore too late to apply for the removal after the pleadings have been read and the evidence submitted, and before the argument has begun.

Where the only objection in the Federal court to the removal is *that the application was not made in the State court in time,* this objection may undoubtedly be *waived* by acquiescence, or even the failure of the other party to make it the ground of an objection to the jurisdiction of the Federal court in proper time; and it will be waived, we

⁹ Lewis v. Smythe (Woods, Circuit Judge), 2 Woods C. C. 117 (1875). Construing the word "trial," as used in section 3 of the act of 1875, in reference to the time when the removal must be applied for, Woods, Circuit Judge, in Lewis v. Smythe, 2 Woods C. C. 117, 118, 119, says: "By the word ·trial.· as used in the statute, I do not understand the argument, investigation or decision of a question of law merely, unless it is decisive of the case, and the question results in a final judgment or decree. The decision of the court on a demurrer, for instance, or on exceptions to the sufficiency of a plea, which is followed by amendments or new pleadings, and which does not end the case, is not the trial meant by the statute." The trial meant is one which "involves the facts of the case: and whenever the investigation of the facts of a case simply, or the facts in connection with the law is entered upon by the court alone, or by the court and jury, the trial may be said to have begun." The petition must be filed not only before "the trial is completed and ended, but before it commences."

Construing the word "trial" in the act of 1875, sec. 3, see Price v. Sommers (North. Dist. Ohio), cited *supra,* 8 Ch. Legal News, 290.

In Ames v. Colorado Central R. R. Co. (Dist. Col.; Dillon & Hallett, JJ.) 4 Cent. L. J. 199. it was ruled, under the act of 1875, that the application to remove a cause must be made to the State court at or before the term in which according to the local law and practice of the court. the cause could have been finally heard. Accordingly where issue was joined nearly one month before the end of a term of the State court, and it does not appear but that a final hearing could have been had at that term. an application thereafter made to remove the cause under the act of 1875 is too late. It was also decided that the act of 1875, which provides that any suit "now pending or hereafter brought in any State court ", of the description therein specified, may be removed into a Federal court, is not applicable to a suit brought in a *Territorial* court, although on the admission of the Territory as a State such suit passed into the jurisdiction of a State court. *Ib.*

think, unless the objection be made by the party entitled to make it, before he takes any affirmative action in the Federal court, or voluntarily submits himself to its action.[90] In one case, the mere failure to move to remand at the same term at which the record was filed, the party making the motion not having taken any steps in the cause after its removal, was held not to preclude making the objection at the next term.[91]

The act of March 3, 1875, sec. 2, extends, *inter alia*, to " *any* suit   *   *   *now pending*;" and by section 3, the petition for removal must be filed in the State court " before or at the term at which said cause could be first tried, and before the trial thereof." It has been contended that the general language of the act "now pending," does not include cases, where prior to the passage of the act a term of the State court had passed, at which the cause might have been tried, though it was not; nor to cases where there had been a trial prior to the passage of that act, and a new trial had been ordered, and the cause was pending for such retrial when the act took effect. But the Federal Circuit courts have uniformly, and we think, properly decided otherwise, and have held that causes which might have been tried before the passage of the act of March 3, 1875, but were not, and which were pending for trial when that act went into operation, as well as causes once tried, but in which a new trial had been ordered, and which were pending, ready for retrial when the act took effect, are re-

---

[90] The objection that the application to remove the cause was not made in time may be *conclusively waived* by submitting to the jurisdiction of the Circuit court by taking testimony and by delaying the objection for an unreasonable time. French v. Hay. 22 Wall. 244; Ames v. Colorado Central R. R. Co. (Dist. Col.), 9 Ch. Legal News, 132. (1876); s. c., 4 Cent. L. J. 199; Young v. Andes Ins. Co., (S. D. Ohio; Swing J.), 3 Cent. L. J. 719. (1876).

[91] See opinion of Yaple. J.. in Kaufman v. McNutt. (Sup. Court of Cin.), 3 Cent. L. J. 408; Kain v. Texas Pacific R. R. Co., (under act of July 27, 1868, East. Dist. Texas, Duval. J.), 3 Cent. L. J. 12 (1875); Carrington v. Florida R. R. Co. (Benedict. J.), 9 Blatchf. 467 (1872).

movable,[92] if the application therefor be made after the passage of the act and within the time therein required.[93]

SECTION XIV.

MODE OF MAKING APPLICATION FOR REMOVAL—BOND, ETC.

Under the Revised Statutes, sec. 639, the applicant for the removal must file his petition therefor, stating the grounds for the removal, and offer in the State court good and sufficient surety for his entering in the Circuit court, on the first day of its next session, copies of the process [proceedings] against him, and of all pleadings, depositions and other proceedings in the cause, etc. This petition is not required to be verified.

Under the act of 1867 (Revised Statutes, sec. 639, subdivision 3). there is required in addition to the petition for removal an *affidavit of prejudice or local influence*, which, wherever possible, should be made by the party himself; or if the petition is on behalf of a corporation, by the president or managing or other proper officer, or by some person authorized to control the case.[94] The decisions upon the

[92] Crane v. Reeder, (Emmons, Circuit Judge), 15 Albany L. J. 103. denying correctness of the contrary decision of the Supreme Court of Michigan. 28 Mich. 527; Andrews, Exec. v. Garrett.(Swing, Dist. Judge), 3 Cent. L. J. 797; s. c. Ch. Legal News (January 8. 1876). p. 132: Mer. and Manuf. Bank v. Wheeler, (Johnson, Circuit Judge). 3 Cent. L. J. 13; Hoadley v. San Francisco, (Sawyer, Circuit Judge), 8 Chicago Legal News, 134. The decisions in the 8th judicial circuit have always been in accordance with this view.

[93] Ames v. Colorado Central R. R. Co., (Dillon & Hallett, JJ.) Feb. 1877, cited *supra*.

[94] See Anon., 1 Dillon, 298. note: Trust Co. v. Maquillan. 3 Dillon. 379, 380, where Mr. Justice Miller is reported as saying: " I am not impressed with the soundness of the argument that, because corporations can not make an affidavit. except through the proper officers, they were not within the contemplation of Congress. I think that the proper officers of corporations may make the necessary affidavit to procure the removal."

The president, and perhaps the general manager of a railway com-

point whether an attorney may make the affidavit in any
case, or what officers of a corporation may make it, are
few.

It is not necessary to state in the affidavit the reasons or
facts showing the local influence or prejudice ; for this is not
a traversable matter either in the State or Federal court.[95]
As the party himself is a non-resident and may not be as
well advised as his local agent or attorney as to the existence of local influence or prejudice, there would seem to be
no reason for requiring the affidavit in all cases to be made
by the party ; and some parties, as infants or persons *non
compos mentis*, could not make it. If an attorney or agent
makes the affidavit, it is good practice to state why it is not
made by the party himself.

Under the act of March 3, 1875, the removal is effected

pany, is *prima facie* authorized to make the required affidavit in such a case.
Minnett v. Milwaukee etc. Railway Co., 3 Dillon C. C. 460 (1875), Nelson, J.; s. c., 13 Alb. Law J. 254. In Kain v. Texas Pacific R. R. Co., 3
Cent. L. J. 12, the petition for removal was verified by the solicitor of the
corporation defendant, authorized to appear and conduct suits for it in
the state of Texas; no question was made as to his authority or right to
file and verify the petition, which was under the act of July 27, 1868.
(Revised Statutes, sec. 640.)

The *superintendent* of a railroad company having, as incident to his
office as such, no authority to represent the company in judicial proceedings, the Supreme Court of Massachusetts decided that such an officer,
unless specially authorized by the corporation, has no power to make the
affidavit of local influence or prejudice required by the act of 1867, and
on this ground held, that the State court rightfully refused to transfer
the cause. Gray, C. J., observed: "The petition may doubtless be
signed, and the affidavit made by some person authorized to represent the corporation. But the authority of any person assuming to represent it must appear. No officer of a corporation, unless specially authorized, has power to bind the corporation, except in the discharge of
his ordinary duties." Mahone v. Manchester etc. R. R. Corp., 111 Mass.
72 (1872).

The *affidavit* of local prejudice or influence under the act of 1867 *may
be taken and certified* in conformity with the laws of the state, as there
is no act of Congress regulating this subject. Bowen v. Chase, 7 Blatchf.
255.

[95] Anon., 1 Dillon, 298, note; Meadow Valley Mine Co. v. Dodds, 7
Nev. 143.

by the proper party making and filing, in the State court, a petition in the suit to be removed, setting forth therein the grounds for the removal. This petition is not required to be verified.[96] Petitions for removal usually state not only the grounds for the removal arising from citizenship or the nature of the subject-matter, but also that the amount in dispute exceeds $500. Where, however, the amount is shown by the pleadings in the case to exceed this sum, it is not necessary, although it is not improper, to make a statement in the petition for the removal as to the sum or value in dispute.[97] The petition for removal should be carefully framed, and in removals under the Revised Statutes, sec. 639, the prudent practitioner will follow the exact language of the statute in stating the grounds for the removal.[98]

It has been decided by some of the State courts that the petition for the removal must expressly state that the parties were citizens of the respective states *at the time the suit was commenced*, and that it is not sufficient to state it in the present tense, or as of the time when the petition for removal was made or filed.[99] This view is open to some doubt. It overlooks the purpose of the Constitution and of Congress in providing for removals, which was to give a resort by the non-resident party to a tribunal in which the citizen of the state should have no advantage over him. It is inconsistent with several adjudications under the latter acts.[100] Whatever may be the law on the point, the careful attorney will state

[96] Connor v. Scott, 3 Cent. L. J. 305; Merchants' etc. Bank v. Wheeler, 3 Cent. L. J. 13, *per* Johnson, Circuit Judge.

[97] Abranches v. Schell, 4 Blatchf. 256; Turton v. U. P. R. R. Co., 3 Dillon. 366.

[98] Railway Co. v. Ramsey, 22 Wall. 328. where the requisites, function and effect of the petition for removal are tersely stated by the Chief Justice. Amory v. Amory, 36 N. Y. Sup. Ct. Rep. 520.

[99] Pechner v. Phœnix Ins. Co., N. Y. Court of Appeals, May. 1875; s. c., 6 Lans. 411; Holden v. Putnam Fire Ins. Co., 46 N. Y. 1; Indianapolis etc. R. R. Co. v. Risley, 50 Ind. 60; Savings Bank v. Benton, 2 Metc. (Ky.) 240; People v. Superior Court, 34 Ill. 356; Tapley v. Martin, 116 Mass. 275 (1874).

[100] Johnson v. Monell. 1 Woolw. 390; McGinnity v. White. 3 Dillon, 350.

in his petition for removal that the plaintiff, when the suit in the State court was commenced, was and still is a citizen of the state in which the suit is brought, etc., etc.

Where it is sought to remove a suit on the ground that it is one " arising under the Constitution, or laws or treaties of the United States," (Act of March 3, 1875, Sec. 2), it should appear from the pleadings or the petition for the removal, or both, that the case is one of this character.[101] If this does not appear from the pleadings, that is, from the averments of facts therein or the nature of the case made thereby, then it must be made to appear by the petition for the removal : and the Circuit Judge for the Ninth Circuit, in a recent opinion where the point is carefully examined, has reached the conclusion, and enforced it by very persuasive arguments arising from the delay, inconvenience and abuse which would follow from a different practice, that the petition for the removal must state the *facts* (unless they appear in the pleadings) which show the case to be one of Federal cognizance, and that it is not sufficient to state generally that the case is one arising under the Constitution or Laws of the United States.[102]

[101] Construction of this clause in act of 1875. See *ante.* sec. 8.

[102] Trafton v. Nougues. 13 Pacific Law Rep., 49; s. c.. 4 Cent. L. J. 228. After stating the delay and obstruction to the administration of justice. which would result from allowing the petitioner for the removal to effect it on his mere statement that the case was one arising under the Constitution or Laws of the United States.—the duty of the Federal court to remand the cause at any stage when its non-federal character appears— the territorial extent of the Federal jurisdiction—the increased cost of litigation in the Federal courts—the abuse of the right by unscrupulous persons, to obtain delay or to harrass their adversary,—Mr. Circuit Judge Sawyer concludes his opinion, in the case just cited, as follows : " In view of these. in my judgment, weighty considerations, therefore, I think it of the highest importance to the rights of honest litigants. and to the due and speedy administration of justice. that a petition for transfer should state the *exact facts,* and distinctly point out what the question is, and how and where it will arise, which gives jurisdiction to the court, so that the court can determine for itself from the facts, whether the suit does really and substantially involve a dispute or con- troversy within its jurisdiction. Whenever, therefore, the record fails to distinctly show such facts in a case transferred to this court, it will be

Surety—Bond.—Under section 639 of the Revised Statutes, good and sufficient surety is to be offered in the State court, at the time of filing the petition for the removal, for the petitioner's " entering in the Circuit court on the first day of its next session copies of the process," etc. This is substantially the requirement in this regard of the act of March 3, 1875, (sec. 3), except that the surety is to be given by a " bond" which is conditioned, not only for the entering of a copy of the record of the State court in the suit, but for "paying all costs that may be awarded by said Circuit court, if said court shall hold that such suit was wrongfully or improperly removed thereto." But if the Circuit court should hold that the suit was removable, it would not, probably, dismiss or remand it, because the bond did not contain this condition as to costs, or was otherwise informal.[103] This section has

returned to the State court, and under the authority given by section 5, at the cost of the party transferring it. If I am wrong in my construction of the act and the recent decisions of the Supreme court, the statute, section 5, happily affords a speedy remedy by writ of error, upon which this decision and the order remanding the case may be reviewed without waiting for a trial, and the question may as well be set at rest in this case as in any other. It is of the utmost importance that a final decision of the question be had as soon as possible. If counsel so desire, I will order the clerk to delay returning the case till they have an opportunity to sue out and perfect a writ of error."

[103] Section 5 of the act of March 3, 1875. The defendants, under the act of 1789, must give several, or joint and several bonds, and not joint bonds,—so held by Potter. J., in Hazard v. Durant, 9 R. I. 602; but *quære?*

A case was remanded by Gresham. J., because the bond did not comply with the act of 1867, the penal sum being left blank, and because it did not contain the conditions required by the act of 1875. Burdeck v. Hale, 8 Ch. L. N., 192 (1876).

Where the party seeking a removal presents a bond apparently ample, the *State court* (assuming that that court may insist upon " a good and sufficient bond") can not arbitrarily refuse to receive the bond, and refuse to remove the case without giving the party an opportunity to correct the bond or make it ample. In an action where the claim was less than $600, and where a bond for $2000, in due form, with two sureties who justified in the sum of $4000 each, was presented, which the court refused to accept, without stating any reasons, the appellate court reversed the judgment, and held that it could not assume, under the cir-

been construed by the learned Circuit Judge of the 7th Circuit, who holds that " it did not intend that the suit should be dismissed or remanded on account of irregularities, provided it satisfactorily appears that the Circuit court has jurisdiction of the case."[104] But if the removal was not applied for in time, this is not treated as an unimportant irregularity, and the uniform practice is to remand the case. This objection must, however, be made seasonably, or it will be deemed waived.[105]

SECTION XV.

EFFECT OF PETITION AND BOND FOR REMOVAL ON THE JURIS-DICTION OF THE STATE COURT.

The removal acts provide that, upon the filing of the proper petition and the offer of good and sufficient surety or bond, " it shall be the duty of the State court to accept the surety," [under act of March 3, 1875, " to accept said petition and bond"] "and to proceed no further in the suit," [under the act of 1866 " no farther in the cause"] " against the petitioner for removal."[106] If the case be within the act of Congress, and the petition is in due form, accompanied with the offer of the required surety or bond, the statute is that the State court *must* accept the surety or the

---

cumstances, that the lower court refused the bond, because not satisfied with the sureties. Taylor v. Shaw, 54 N. Y. (Ct. of Appeals), 75 (1873.)

[104] Osgood v. Chicago, etc., R. R. Co., 7 Ch. Legal News, 241; s. c. 2 Cent. L. J. 275, and. on re-argument. 2 Cent. L. J. 283. See, also, Parker v. Overman, 18 How. 137, 141: *Infra*, sec. 15.

[105] French v. Hay, 22 Wall. 244: *Supra*, sec. 13.

[106] Rev. Stats., sec. 639. It is doubtful whether parties can *remove a cause by a stipulation* of the jurisdictional facts. At all events the practice should not be encouraged; and where a minor was a party, it was held he was incapable of consenting to the removal, and the cause was remanded. Kingsbury v. Kingsbury, 3 Bissell. 60 (1871), Davis, Drummond and Blodgett, JJ.. concurring.

petition and bond, and proceed no further in the case. Under such circumstances the State court has no power to refuse the removal, and can do nothing to affect the right, and its *rightful* jurisdiction ceases *eo instanti;* no order for the removal is necessary, and every subsequent exercise of jurisdiction by the State court, including its judgment, if one is rendered, is erroneous.[107] And if the right of removal

[107] Fisk v. Union Pacific Railroad Co., 6 Blatchf. 362; s. c., *ib.* 243, 299; Hatch v. Chicago, Rock Island & Pacific Railroad Co., 6 *ib.* 105; Matthews v. Lyall, 6 McLean, 13. The petition or application "for removal is *ex parte*, and depends upon the papers on which it is founded, and if they are regular and conform to the requirements of the statute, the [State] court has no discretion "—and the adverse party is not entitled to notice of the time and place of presenting the petition. Fisk v. Union Pacific Railroad Co. (Nelson, J.), 8 Blatchf. 243, 247 (1871).

"In cases where the proceedings are in conformity with the act, the removal is imperative, both upon the State and Circuit court; and if the facts [upon which the removal is based] are seriously contested, it must be done in a formal manner, by pleadings and proofs, in the latter court. The question of jurisdiction [in such a case] belongs to the Federal court, and must be heard and determined there." Nelson, J., in Dennistoun v. Draper, 5 Blatchf. 336, 338 (1866).

No *order* of removal necessary. Hatch v. C., R. I. & P. R. R. Co., 6 Blatchf. 105 (1868).

Petition for removal was founded on the act of 1867. It did not show a right under this act, but did state a case within the act of 1866, and it was held sufficient to require a removal so far as authorized by the last-named act. Dart v. Walker, 4 Daly (N. Y.), 188 (1871).

"Where a suit is legally removed," says Gray, C. J., "into the Circuit court of the United States, the jurisdiction of the State courts over it ceases, and the suit is thenceforth to proceed to trial, judgment and execution in the Federal courts, and can not be remanded to the State courts for any purpose. Kanouse v. Martin, 15 How. 198; Ins. Co. v. Dunn, 19 Wall. 214; Mahone v. Manchester etc. R. R. Co., 111 Mass. 72. Such removal of a case from the State to the Federal courts for trial does not change the nature of the issue to be tried or the judgment to be rendered. West v. Aurora, 6 Wall. 139; Partridge v. Ins. Co., 15 Wall. 573." Du Vivier v. Hopkins, 116 Mass. 125, 128.

In the text we use the phrase "the *rightful* jurisdiction ceases *eo instanti*," and a subsequent judgment of the State court "is erroneous,"— we do not say null and void. Such a judgment is perhaps valid, unless reversed or set aside; but in many of the cases every subsequent exercise of jurisdiction is said to be null and void, and every step *coram non judice.* How far the subsequent proceedings in the State court have any validity, if a proper application for removal be refused, see Herryford v. Ætna

has once become perfect, it can not be taken away by sub-sequent amendment in the State court or Federal court, or by a release of part of the debt or damages claimed, or otherwise.[108]

Ins. Co., 42 Mo. 151, 153, where it is said "they are *coram non judice;*" S. P. Akerly v. Vilas, 1 Abb. U. S. 284; s. c., 2 Bissell, 110; Fisk v. Union Pacific R. R. Co., 6 Blatchf. 362; s. c., 8 *ib.* 243, 299; Stevens v. Phœnix Ins. Co., 41 N. Y. 149; and compare with Kanouse v. Martin, 15 How. 198; Gordon v. Longest, 16 Pet. 97; Ins. Co. v. Dunn, 19 Wall. 214; French v. Hay, 22 Wall. 250; Amory v. Amory, 36 N. Y. Superior Ct. R. 520; Bell v. Dix, 49 N. Y. 232; Stanley v. Ch.. R. I. & P. R. R. Co. (Sup. Ct. of Mo.), 3 Cent. L. J. 430 (1876); Hadley v. Dunlap, 10 Ohio St. 1, 8, where the matter is discussed by Scott, J.; DuVivier v. Hopkins, 116 Mass. 125, 126.

The doctrine of the text to the effect that. if the petition for the re-moval presents a case within the removal acts, and is made in due time and accompanied with the proper surety, no *order* for the removal is necessary, is very strongly combated by Chancellor Cooper in the SOUTHERN LAW REVIEW for April, 1877. This learned writer contends that under such circumstances the jurisdiction of the State court contin-ues, " until it has finally parted with it by the necessary order." and per consequence, that the Circuit court can in no case acquire jurisdiction, unless the State court has ordered the removal. No authority is cited for this position, except the case of the Railway Co. v. Ramsey, 22 Wall. 328, which it is a mistake to suppose *decided* any such proposition; and the Chief Justice. in the language referred to, probably had no such thought in his mind. The doctrine that an *order* of removal in such a case is not necessary to the jurisdiction of the Circuit court is universally accepted in those courts, and is constantly acted on. The acts of Con-gress speak of no order of removal being necessary; some of the acts distinctly provide for the cases proceeding in the Federal court, notwith-standing the State court or clerk may refuse to send or furnish copies of the record; and the act of 1875 (sec. 7) provides for a writ of *certiorari* to enforce not only the removal of a cause which the State court has or-dered to be removed, but of any cause " removable under the act," where the parties entitled to a removal " have complied with the provisions of this act for the removal of the same." It would contravene the plain purpose of this provision to hold that a *certiorari* could rightfully issue only in cases where the State court had ordered the removal, or that it would be an answer to the writ for the State court to return that it had refused to order the removal.

[108] Kanouse v. Martin (amendment), 15 How. 198; s. c., 1 Blatchf. 149; Ladd v. Tudor, 3 Woodb. & Minot, 325; Muns v. Dupont, 2 Wash. C. C. 463; Akerly v. Vilas. 1 Abb. U. S. 284; s. c., 2 Bissell, 110; Hatch v. Rock Island etc. R. R. Co., 6 Blatchf. 105; Fisk v. Union Pacific R. R. Co., 6 *ib.* 362; s. c.. 8 *ib.* 243; Roberts v. Nelson (amount), 8 *ib.* 74;

If the petition in connection with the pleadings does not show that the case is removable, the jurisdiction of the State court is not ousted, and its subsequent proceedings, if it refused to order the removal, would not, it is supposed, be void or erroneous.[108]

And the same principle would apply, probably, if *no security* or bond whatever was offered and no removal ordered, since in that event the prescribed conditions for the removal have not been complied with ; but it is doubtful, especially under the act of 1875, whether it belongs to the State court to judge of the sufficiency of the surety offered, and to refuse a removal because the surety or bond is not sufficient, and exercise jurisdiction subsequently on that ground alone.[110]

In the case of Osgood v. Chicago etc. R. R. Co.,[111] the petition and bond for the removal of the cause were filed in the vacation of the State court with the clerk, and it was

Gordon v. Longest. 16 Pet. 97; Matthews v. Lyall (as to right to dismiss), 6 McLean. 13; Wright v. Wells. Pet. C. C. 220; Stanley v. C.. R. I. & P. R. R. Co.. 3 Cent. L. J. 430.

[108] Gordon v. Longest, 16 Pet. 97; Ins. Co. v. Dunn, 19 Wall. 214; Kanouse v. Martin, 14 How. 23; s. c., 15 How. 198; Stevens v. Phœnix Ins. Co., 41 N. Y. 149; Holden v. Putnam Fire Ins. Co., 46 N. Y. 1; Savings Bank v. Benton. 2 Metc. (Ky.) 240.

[110] See *nisi prius* opinion of Morton, J., in Bank v. King Wrought Iron Bridge Co., 2 Cent. L. J. 505, denying Osgood v. Chicago etc. R. R. Co., *infra* ; s. c. in Circuit court U. S., 2 Cent. L. J. 616. See *Ib.*, 679, 730. The ruling of Drummond, J., in Osgood's case, approved Jones v. Amazon Ins. Co., 9 Ch. Legal News, 68. dissented from in Mayo v. Taylor. 8 Ch. Legal News, 11. See also *dictum* of the Chief Justice in Railway Co. v. Ramsey, 22 Wall.328, that '' if upon *the hearing* of the petition it is sustained by proof, the State court can proceed no further '' —but *quære*, whether the State court can hear and determine whether the proofs sustain the petition.

Mr. Chancellor Cooper, in the SOUTHERN LAW REVIEW for April 1877, combats the doctrine of Judge Drummond in the Osgood Case and the other cases that follow it, namely, that the State court has no right to pass upon the sufficiency of the bond. The point is by no means clear, and there is reason (looking at the object of the bond and the language of the act of Congress) for the opinion, that it was contemplated that the State court might reject a bond distinctly on the ground that it was not sufficient; but its action in this regard can not be admitted to be conclusive, *in all cases*, on the Federal courts.

[111] 2 Cent. L. J. 275; s. c., 7 Ch. Legal News, 241.

held that this, without any action of the court as to the sufficiency of the petition or bond, *ipso facto*, deprived the State
court of jurisdiction—the sufficiency of these (under the act
of 1875) being for the Circuit court. Judge Drummond says :
" It is true that under the statute the bond must be good and
sufficient security ; but it does not declare that it shall be
approved by the judge. It requires the State court to accept the petition and bond, and proceed no further in the
case.[112] The fifth section of the act of March 3, 1875, tends
to confirm the view that the State court is not authorized
to make a judicial inquiry into and decision on the sufficiency
of the *bond*. Its determination, however, that a *sufficient
petition* is not sufficient, can not deprive the Federal court
of jurisdiction. So its determination that an *insufficient
petition* is sufficient, while it is not immaterial, especially if
accompanied with an order for removal, will not conclude
that question, and it will be the duty of the Federal court,
on motion, to remand the cause.[113]

SECTION XVI.

EFFECT ON THE JURISDICTION OF THE FEDERAL COURT.

" Upon the copy of the record of the suit being entered
as aforesaid in the Circuit court of the United States," the
provision is, " that the cause shall then proceed in the same
manner as if it had been originally commenced in the said
Circuit court." " And the copies of the pleadings shall
have the same force and effect, in every respect and for every
purpose, as the *original pleadings* would have had by the
laws and practice of the courts of the State, if the cause had
remained in the State court.'"[114]

[112] See 2 Cent. L. J. 616.
[113] Urtetiqui v. D'Arcy, 9 Pet. 692.
[114] Rev. Stats., sec. 639. And see act March 3, 1875, secs. 3, 6.

No *new pleadings* are in general necessary in the cause after its removal to the Federal court,[115] though it may often be advisable, especially in equity cases, to file new pleadings. We have before referred to this subject.[116] The *practice* after removal is to be the same, as if the cause had been originally brought in the Federal court, including the power to allow amendments.[117] *Amendments* in respect to jurisdictional facts have sometimes been allowed.[118]

The jurisdiction of the Circuit court does not, probably, attach until the record of the State court is entered therein. If it be entered *before* the time, it has been made a question whether it will *then* attach. For some purposes it would seem that it might; as, for example, if it became necessary meanwhile to issue an injunction or appoint a receiver (which should be done, however, only upon notice), in order to protect the rights of the parties or to preserve the property in litigation.

By express provision of *existing statutes*, *attachments* of property hold, *bonds* of indemnity remain valid, and writs of *injunction* continue in force notwithstanding the re-

[115] Dart v. McKinney (act of 1866), 9 Blatchf. 359 (1872), Blatchford, J. *Supra*, sec. 9 and cases cited. In removals under the Judiciary Act, the defendant is not in default for not pleading in the State court, and he may plead in the Circuit court. Webster v. Crothers, 1 Dillon C. C. 301 (1870).

[116] *Supra*, sec. 9 and cases there cited.

[117] Suydam v. Ewing, 2 Blatchf. 359 (1852). Betts, J.; Akerly v. Vilas, 5 Ch. Legal News, 73; *supra*, sec. 9 and cases cited.

[118] In the original petition the plaintiff, by mistake of his attorney, described himself as a citizen of the state where the suit was brought; he obtained a removal of the case on the ground that he was a citizen of another state, and in the Federal court he was permitted by Mr. Justice Bradley to amend his petition and state his true citizenship, both then, and when the suit was commenced, and to make new parties defendant with respect to matters properly pertaining to the original cause of action. Barclay v. Levee Commissioners, 1 Woods C. C. 254. In Hodgson v. Bowerbank, 5 Cranch, 303, the court having decided that the objection to the jurisdiction (the defendant being described in the record as "late of the District of Maryland," instead of a *citizen* of Maryland) was fatal, the "record was afterwards amended by consent." Parker v. Overman, 18 How. 137, cited *infra*, sec. 17, note.

moval, until dissolved or modified by the Circuit court.[119]
This provision was, doubtless, enacted to obviate a different judicial construction which has been placed upon
previous removal acts.[120]

SECTION XVII.

REMANDING OF CAUSE TO THE STATE COURT.

If the petition for the removal and the copy of the
pleadings or record in the State court, taken together, do not
show that the case was removable under the legislation of
Congress ; or if they show that the removal was not applied
for in time ; or that any other substantial condition of the
right of removal, such as value, has not been met or complied with, but the removal has, nevertheless, been ordered,
the other party may move to remand the cause to the State
court, and it ought to be remanded accordingly.   This was

[119] Rev. Stats., sec. 646: Act March 3, 1875, sec. 4.

[120] See New England Screw Co. v. Bliven, 3 Blatchf. 240, but *quære?*
Barney v. Globe Bank (*attachment* holds the property after removal under
the Judiciary Act, sec. 12), 5 Blatchf. 107 (1862).

Attachment—Motion to Dissolve.—A motion to dissolve an attachment
when authorized by the local laws, may be made in the Circuit court after
the removal; and in the discretion of the court it may be renewed, although it was once argued and denied in the State court.   Garden City
Manuf. Co. v. Smith, 1 Dillon C. C. 305 (1870).   As to custody and dis-
position of property attached, Dennistoun v. Draper, 5 Blatchf. 336.

Injunction—Motion to Dissolve.—Under the act of July 13, 1866 (14
Stats. at Large, 171, sec. 67), Drummond, Circuit Judge, following the
decision of McLean, J., in McLeod v. Duncan, 5 McLean, 342, held that
an injunction issued by the State court was *ipso facto* dissolved by the removal of the cause into the Federal court—that act making provision that
" all attachments made, and all bail and security given upon such suit or
prosecution, shall continue in force," and saying nothing as to injunctions.   See Hatch v. Chicago, R. I. & P. R. R. Co., 6 Blatchf, 105, holding same doctrine as to cases removed under sec. 12 of the Judiciary
Act.   But these decisions are no longer applicable, where there is an express statute provision, that injunctions granted by the State court continue in force after the removal of the cause, until dissolved or modified

the uniform practice before the act of 1875 ; but under the 5th section of that act, while it is clear that a cause ought to be remanded which is not removable, or in which the right to a removal has been waived because not applied for in time, and the like, it is doubtful whether, if the record was in fact filed in the Federal court in time, defects connected with the giving of the surety or bond, or other irregularities which have not worked any prejudice, will be ground for dismissing or remanding the case.[121]

The section last referred to makes it the duty of the Circuit court to dismiss or remand the case whenever it appears, to its satisfaction, that the " suit does not really and substantially involve a dispute or controversy properly within the jurisdiction of the Circuit court." In our judgment this is the test of Federal jurisdiction, and the one which ought to be applied to the complex and diversified cases which will arise under the act of 1875, namely, if the *real and substantial* controversy is one between citizens of different states, although incidentally and collaterally there may be a controversy between some parties who may be citizens of the same state ; or if the case is one which arises under the Constitution or Laws of the United States, although not wholly depending thereon as before explained, the case is one of Federal cognizance and should be retained ; otherwise, dismissed or remanded.

A party entitled to a removal may estop himself to apply

by the Federal court. Where an injunction has been allowed by the State court upon a full hearing, and the cause is afterwards removed,—while the Federal court may, under the act of 1866, dissolve the injunction, yet, where the *motion to dissolve is upon the same papers* on which the writ was granted (this being in effect an application for re-argument of the motion made in the State court), leave to make such motion should first be applied for and obtained, before it can be made. Carrington v. Florida R. R. Co., 9 Blatch. 468 (1872). Benedict, J.

121 See *supra*, sec. 9, as to *time* of applying for removal. When the case is one of Federal cognizance, the right to have the cause remanded, because of defects in mode of removal, etc., may be waived. But there is no waiver of the right, where the case is not really and substantially one of Federal jurisdiction. Price v. Sommers, 8 Ch. Legal News, 290.

for it,[122] or, having applied, may waive the right to a removal by his subsequent conduct in the State court ;[123] but contesting the case in the State court, after it has erroneously refused to grant the application for a removal, is no waiver of the party's right.[124]

Under sec. 639 of the Revised Statutes, and under the act of 1875, the defendant must give surety for his *entering copies of the record* on "the first day of the next session" of the Federal court—the latter act providing further (sec. 7), that if the next term shall commence within twenty days after the application for removal, the party shall have twenty days, from the time of the application, to file in the Federal court the copy of the record and enter his appearance therein. If this condition of the undertaking and bond is not complied with, the obligors would doubtless be liable on the bond ; and there may be such unexcused laches in the filing of the copy of the record of the State court, as where without necessity or good reason a term lapses, or the other party is prejudiced by the delay, that the Federal court will for this reason remand the case, even though it be one of Federal cognizance. Such is the practice of the Federal courts, so far as we are acquainted with it.[125]

---

[122] Executing bond to procure discharge from a writ of *ne exeat*, held to *estop*, by its condition " to abide the decree of the State court"—the defendant who executed it. to remove the cause to the Federal court. Hazard v. Durant *et al.* (Potter, J.), 9 Rhode Island, 602, 606 (1868).

[123] A petition and bond for removal were filed in the State court;—no motion was made or entered. nor the attention of the court called to the fact, and the parties nearly a year afterwards went to trial on the merits. On appeal the court held. that *the right to a removal could be waived*, and under the circumstances must be considered waived; though it was admitted that it would have been otherwise. if the court had been cognizant of the petition, and that the party insisted on it. and had nevertheless ordered the trial to proceed. Home Ins. Co. v. Curtis (Sup. Ct. Mich.), 3 Cent. L. J. 27 (1875).

[124] Insurance Co. v. Dunn. 19 Wall. 214; Gordon v. Longest, 16 Pet. 98; Kanouse v. Martin. 15 How. 198; Stevens v. Phœnix Ins. Co., 41 N. Y. 149; Hadley v. Dunlap. 10 Ohio St. 1.

[125] *Supra*, sec. 14. *Time of filing copies of papers.* Where the petition for

The *motion to remand must be based* upon the petition for
removal and the record as it is sent up from the State court.
If the petition, in connection with the record, is sufficient
on its face, but states as ground of removal facts which
are not true, as for example, in regard to citizenship, or
value, where the value does not appear in the pleadings,
issue may be taken thereon in the Circuit court by a plea in
the nature of a plea in abatement ;[126] but such an inquiry
can not be gone into in the State court.[127]

Where the State court has ordered the removal improp-

removal was filed in February, 1874, and the next term of the Federal
court was in April, 1874, and copies of the proper papers were not filed
until August, 1875, the delay was such that the Federal court remanded
the case, and held that the delay was not excused by the action of the State
court in denying the petition, and the petitioner's action in the mean-
time in securing, by appeal to the state appellate tribunal, a reversal of the
order denying the removal. Clippinger v. Mo. Valley Life Ins. Co.
(North. Dist. Ohio), 8 Chicago Legal News. 115 (1875); but *quære*,
whether under the circumstances the delay was not sufficiently excused.

[126] Coal Co. v. Blatchford, 11 Wall. 172; Heath v. Austin, 12 *ib.* 320.
"The motion to remand admits the facts set out in the petition for removal, and proceeds upon the ground that under the state of facts [pre-
sented in the record] the case was improperly removed, and this court
is without jurisdiction over it." Buttner v. Miller, 1 Woods C. C. 620
(1871). When motion to remand is proper, and when not. Heath v.
Austin, 12 Blatchf. 320; Dennistoun v. Draper, 5 *ib.* 336; Galvin v.
Boutwell, 9 *ib.* 470.

If the case is *not one of Federal cognizance*, it must be dismissed or re-
manded at any stage when the fact appears or is duly established.
Dennistoun v. Draper, 5 Blatchf. 336 (1856), Nelson, J.; Pollard v.
Dwight, 4 Cranch, 421; Wood v. Matthews, 2 Blatchf. 370.

The act of March 3, 1875, section 5, provides that, if "at any time "
after the removal the non-federal character of the case shall appear,
"the Circuit court *shall* proceed no further therein, but shall dismiss the
suit or remand it to the court from which it was removed, as justice
may require."

[127] Fisk v. Union Pacific R. R., 8 Blatchf. 243 (1871), Nelson, J.; Stewart v. Mordecai, 40 Ga. 1. It is settled law that the facts stated as the
ground of the removal can not be contested or inquired into in the State
court. That inquiry belongs exclusively to the Federal court.

In Knickerbocker Life Ins. Co. v. Gorbach., 70 Pa. St. 150 (1871), both
parties seemed to concede the right of the State court to determine
whether the facts stated in the petition for removal were true, and that
question was tried and decided against the party applying for the re-

erly, the Circuit court should remand the suit.[128] If the State court has remitted the case, though erroneously, its jurisdiction is at an end until it is restored by the action of the Federal courts.[129] If the Circuit court erroneously refuses to remand such a case, the proper remedy of the party is not by proceeding in the State court at the same time the cause is in the Circuit court, but is alone in the Federal court ; the action of the Circuit court in remanding, or refusing to remand, a cause being reviewable on error or appeal by the Supreme Court.[130]

moval, and the decision reversed by the Supreme Court of the State; but this practice is in direct conflict with the acts of Congress in this behalf.

Burden of proof as to jurisdictional facts, where contest is made in the Federal court after the removal. Heath v. Austin, 12 Blatchf. 320.

[128] Act March 3, 1875, sec. 5, referred to *supra*. Although the State court has ordered the removal. yet if such order was improperly made, the Circuit court should remand the cause. as it must determine for itself the question of jurisdiction. Field v. Lownsdale; 1 Deady, 288, Deady, J. Where the Federal court orders a cause remanded to the State court, the Supreme Court of the State will not issue a writ of *mandamus* or other process to restrain the State court from proceeding with the cause, until the party who attempted to transfer the cause to the Federal court can invoke the revisory power of the Supreme Court of the United States to compel such transfer. *Ex parte* State Ins. Co. of Ala., 50 Ala. 464 (1874).

[129] On the order of the Circuit court remanding a cause which the State court had previously ordered to be transferred. the jurisdiction of the latter court re-attaches. and it may proceed therewith. Thacher v. McWilliams. 47 Ga. 306 (1872). But under the act of March 3, 1875 (sec. 5). such an order of the Circuit court is reviewable by the Supreme Court of the United States on appeal or writ of error; and if the order be superseded, a question may arise as to the power of the State court pending the appeal or writ of error. to proceed with the cause under or in consequence of the order remanding it.

[130] Ins. Co. v. Dunn, 19 Wall. 214, 223; Gordon v. Longest. 16 Pet. 97; Act March 3, 1875, sec. 5; Green v. Custard. 23 How. 484; Fasnacht v. Frank (effect of appeal), U. S. Sup. Court, Oct. Term, 1874, 23 Wall. 416. See 2 Cent. L. J. 290.

Where in a suit removed into the Circuit court the papers were afterwards destroyed by fire. and the parties stipulated in writing that the cause was transferred *in accordance with the statute in such case provided*, the Supreme Court will presume. in the absence of proof to the contrary. that the citizenship requisite to give jurisdiction was shown in some proper manner, though it did not appear on the face of the pleadings. R. R.

Where the State court asserts jurisdiction after a proper application for removal, the question of jurisdiction is not waived by the party entitled to the removal, by reason of his appearing and contesting in the State court the claim or matter in dispute.[131] If in such case the judgment of the State court be against him on the trial or hearing, he may appeal to the highest court of the state; and if the decision below is there affirmed, he may sue out a writ of error from the Supreme Court of the United States; and if the record shows that the removal of the suit was improperly denied, that court will not examine into the merits of the case or generally into the record, but will reverse the judgment of the highest court of the state, with directions to reverse the judgment of the lower State court and to order a transfer of the cause from that court to the Circuit court of the United States, pursuant to the petition for the removal originally filed in such State court.[132] The Circuit court has the power

Co. v. Ramsey, 22 Wall. 322. In a petition for removal it was stated that the parties "resided" in such and such states. The Supreme Court said: "'Citizenship' and 'residence' are not synonymous terms; but as the record [in the Circuit court] was afterwards so amended as to show conclusively the citizenship of the parties, the court below had, and this court have, undoubted jurisdiction of the case." Parker v. Overman, 18 How. 137, 141. Amendments, see *supra*, sec. 16 and cases cited.

An averment, that the party defendant is a citizen of the Southern District of Alabama, is a sufficient averment that he is a citizen of Alabama. Berlin v. Jones, 1 Woods C. C. 638.

[131] Ins. Co. v. Dunn, 19 Wall. 214; Gordon v. Longest, 16 Pet. 98; Kanouse v. Martin, 15 How. 198; Stevens v. Phœnix Ins. Co., 41 N. Y. 149; Hadley v. Dunlap, 10 Ohio St. 1; Stanley v. C., R. I. & P. R. R. Co., 3 Cent. L. J. 430.

[132] Gaines v. Fuentes, Sup. Court U. S. Oct. Term, 1875, 2 Otto, 10; s. c., 3 Cent. L. J. 371, and see cases last cited. In the Atlas Ins. Co. v. Byrus, 45 Ind. 133 (1873), the State court of original jurisdiction improperly refused to transfer the cause to the Federal court, and rendered judgment against the party entitled to the removal:—on appeal, the Supreme Court of the State reversed the judgment and remanded the cause to the court below, with directions to sustain the application to remove the cause to the Circuit court of the United States.

The State courts have generally held, that *an appeal lies to the appellate court of the state* from an order for the removal of a cause to a Federal court, or from an order referring such removal. State v. The

to protect its suitors by injunction against a judgment in the
Judge, 23 La. An. 29 (1871); Bryant v. Rich. 106 Mass. 180; Crane v.
Reeder, 28 Mich. 527 (1874); Whiton v. Chicago & N. W. R. R. Co., 25
Wis. 424: s. c.. 13 Wall. 270; Darst v. Bates, 51 Ill. 439.   See opinion of
Gray, C. J.. in Mahone v. Manchester etc. R. R. Co., 111 Mass. 74; Hough v.
West. Transp. Co.,1 Bissell, 425. But the courts In New York have decided
otherwise.   Stevens v. Phœnix Ins. Co., 41 N. Y. 149; Bell v. Dix, 49
N. Y. 232.   See on this subject Ellerman v. New Orleans etc. R. R. Co.,
2 Woods C. C. 120 (1875) (Woods, Circuit Judge); Ins. Co. v. Dunn, 19
Wall 214; Ins. Co. v. Morse, 20 Wall. 445, and cases cited *infra*.

But whatever may be the true view on this point, it is plain that, if the
case is removable, and the application is in due form and in time, the act
of Congress gives " an unqualified and unrestrained right to a removal,"
and declares that the State court shall " proceed no further in the suit;"
and in such a case the State court, it seems plain, can not, after such
application, allow an appeal to the appellate court of the state, and accept a *supersedeas* bond, which shall have the effect to prevent a removal
to the Federal court pending such appeal.   See Akerly v. Vilas, 1
Abb. U. S. Rep. 284.   This is undoubtedly the law under the act of 1875,
which authorizes the Federal court to issue a *certiorari* to the State
court, to which it would not be sufficient for the State court to return
that an appeal had been taken to the appellate court of the state.   Ellerman v. New Orleans R. R. Co., (Woods, Circuit Judge), 2 Woods
C. C. 120 (1875); Insurance Co. v. Morse, 20 Wall. 445.

If a removal has been applied for and denied, and the party persists in
proceeding in the State court, Allen, J.. in Bell v. Dix, 49 N. Y. 232
(1872), conceding that the question of jurisdiction must be decided
by the Federal Circuit Court, said, *arguendo,* that the remedy of the
party, who sought the removal which the State court denied, was to apply to the Circuit court of the United States for the proper mandate
staying proceedings in the State court, and to compel a transcript of the
record to be certified to the Federal court.   If the other party claims
that the cause has not, for any reason, been effectually removed, he
should apply to the Federal court to remand the cause; but the majority
of the court concurred in affirming the order of the special term denying
the motion of the party who sought the removal, to stay in the State
court further proceedings in the action.   In Fisk v. Union Pacific R. R.
Co.. 6 Blatchf. 362, it was held that the Federal court would not, after
the removal of the cause into it, stay proceedings in the State court,
these being null and void.   The ground of these determinations evi-
dently is, that if the removal was properly applied for, it was useless to
stay the proceedings in the State court, as it was deprived of jurisdiction—that is, of rightful jurisdiction; on the other hand, if the removal
was not authorized, it would be improper to interfere with the jurisdiction of the State court.   This conclusion largely rests upon the deli-
cacy with which one court interferes with the proceedings of another,
and leads to no little confusion, expense and embarrassment in its

State court rendered subsequent to a proper application to remove the cause.[133]

If a cause be improperly removed into the Circuit court, and it entertains jurisdiction in a case in which by law it can have none, its judgment will be reversed by the Supreme Court, with directions to the Circuit court to remand the same to the State court whence it was improperly taken.[134]

practical effect. For example, recently, in a case in Iowa, a removal of a cause was sought in the State court. The State court denied it. A copy of the record in the cause was filed in the United States Circuit court for Iowa. That court held that the removal was effectual; the other party appeared, and, on the final hearing, a decree was rendered against him. The State court proceeded with the cause and, on final hearing, rendered a decree in favor of the other party. On appeal to the Supreme Court of the state, it affirmed the judgment below, so that there are two opposite final decrees, one in the State court, and the other in the Federal court—the result of the one court not interfering with the other. The case of French v. Hay, 22 Wall. 250, shows that the Federal court may protect a party by injunction against a judgment in the State court rendered therein after a proper application to remove the cause.

As to appeals from the decision of the *nisi prius* State court granting or refusing the petition for removal to *the appellate court of the state*, and the effect thereof, see, Kanouse v. Martin, 15 How. 198, s. c. 14 How. 23; s. c., 1 Blatchf. 149; Burson v. Park Bank, 40 Ind. 173; Western Union Telegraph Co. v. Dickinson, 40 Ind. 444; Indianapolis etc. R. R. Co. v. Risley, 50 Ind. 60; Whiton v. R. R. Co., 25 Wis. 424; Railroad Co. v. Whiton, 13 Wall. 270; Akerly v. Vilas, 24 Wis. 165; s. c., 2 Bissell, 110; Home Ins. Co. v. Dunn, 20 Ohio St. 175; Ins. Co. v. Dunn, 19 Wall. 214; Atlas Ins. Co. v. Byrns, 45 Ind. 133; Gordon v. Longest, 16 Pet. 97; Hadley v. Dunlap, 10 Ohio St. 1; Stevens v. Phœnix Ins. Co., 41 N. Y. 149; Holden v. Putnam Ins. Co., 46 N. Y. 1; People v. Sup. Court. 34 Ill. 356; Savings Bank v. Benton, 2 Mete. (Ky.) 240; Taylor v. Shaw, 54 N. Y. 75 (1873); Bell v. Dix (interesting case), 49 N. Y. 232 (1872). In case of removal from State to United States court, when the proceedings for removal are regular, the jurisdiction of the State court is *ipso facto* ousted by virtue of such proceedings. The allegation as to jurisdiction can be proven on the trial, and the proper judgment asked for. Shaft v. Phœnix Mut. Life Ins. Co., N. Y. Ct. of Appeals, not yet reported.

[133] French v. Hay, 22 Wall. 250.
[134] Knapp v. Railroad Co., 20 Wall. 117.

APPENDIX.

FORMS OF PETITIONS FOR REMOVAL AND BONDS UNDER THE REVISED STATUTES, SEC. 639, AND THE ACT OF MARCH 3, 1875. FORM OF WRIT OF CERTIORARI AUTHORIZED BY SEC. 7 OF THE LAST-NAMED STATUTE.

The following Forms, with slight alterations, are those in common use in the Eighth Judicial Circuit. By reference to the text it will be seen that they are in some respects unnecessarily full; but they are perhaps safer than others would be, which should be reduced to the exact requirements of the act in the particular case.

Form of PETITION *for the transfer of a cause from the State to the Federal court under the act of March 2, 1867, as revised and embodied in the Revised Statutes of the United States, sec. 639, sub-division 3.*

IN THE ——— COURT OF ——— COUNTY, STATE OF ———.

vs. } Petition for Transfer of Suit to Federal Court.

To the Honorable, the ——— Court of ——— County, State of ——— :

Your petitioner [here insert the plaintiff's name], respectfully shows that he is plaintiff in the foregoing entitled suit, and that the same was by him commenced on or about the —— day of ——, 18 , in said ——— Court; that your petitioner was at the time of bringing said suit, and still is, a citizen of the State of ———, and a resident thereof.

Your petitioner further shows that there is, and was at the time said suit was brought, a controversy therein between your petitioner and the said defendant, ———————, who is a citizen of the State of ———, and resident

6

thereof; that said action was brought by your petitioner, for the pur
pose of [here briefly state the nature of the suit and the relief asked],
and that the matter in dispute in this suit exceeds the sum of five hundred dollars, exclusive of costs. Your petitioner further represents,
that this suit has not been tried, but is now pending for trial in the District court of the State of ——, for said County of ——, and that your
petitioner desires to remove the same into the Circuit court of the
United States for the District of ——, in pursuance of the act of Congress in that behalf provided, to wit, the Revised Statutes of the United
States, section 639, sub-division 3.

Your petitioner further says, that he has filed the affidavit required
by the statute in such cases, and offers herewith his bond executed
by ————, of ——, as surety, in the penal sum of two hundred and
fifty dollars, conditioned as by said act of Congress required.

Your petitioner therefore prays, that the said bond may be accepted as
good and sufficient, according to the said act of Congress, and that the
said suit may be removed into the next Circuit court of the United
States, in and for said District of ——, pursuant to the aforesaid act of
Congress, in such case made and provided; and that no further proceedings may be had therein in this court.

And your petitioner will ever pray, etc.,

Attorney for Plaintiff.

Form of AFFIDAVIT OF PREJUDICE *or local influence to ac-*
company the preceding petition.

IN THE —— COURT OF —— COUNTY, STATE OF ——.

vs.	Plaintiffs. ⎫ ⎬ Affidavit. Defendants. ⎭

State of ——, County of ——. *ss.*

I, ————, being duly sworn, do say that I am one of the————
in the above entitled cause; that I have reason to believe, and do believe, that from prejudice and local influence, ———— will not be able
to obtain justice in said State Court.

Subscribed by the said ———— in my presence, and by him sworn
to before me at ——, this —— day of ——, A. D. 187 .

Notary Public in and for —— County.

Who may make this affidavit. See *ante*, sec. 14. How
to be taken and certified. See *ante*, sec. 14.

Form of BOND *to accompany the Preceding Petition for Removal of a Cause, under the Act of March 2, 1867, as Revised and Embodied in the Revised Statutes of the United States.*

KNOW ALL MEN BY THESE PRESENTS:

That we ——— as principal, and ——— of —— as surety, are hereby held and firmly bound unto ———— in the penal sum of ——— —— Dollars, lawful money of the United States, for the payment of which, well and truly to be made, we bind ourselves jointly and severally firmly by these presents.

The condition of this obligation is such, that if ——— shall enter and file, or cause to be entered and filed, in the next Circuit of the United States, in and for the —— District of ——, on the first day of its session, copies of all process, pleadings, depositions, testimony and other proceedings in a certain suit or action now pending in the District court of the County of —— and State of ——, in which ——— is plaintiff, and ——— defendant; and shall do such other appropriate acts as, by the act of Congress in that behalf, are required to be done upon the removal of such suit from said State court into the said United States court, then this obligation to be void, otherwise of force.

Dated ———, A. D. 187 .

——————————————————
——————————————————

STATE OF ——. }
—— County. } ss.

I, ——— of said County, the surety named in the foregoing bond, being duly sworn, do depose and say that I am a resident of the State of ——, and a property-holder therein; that I am worth the sum of five hundred dollars, over and above all my debts and liabilities, and exclusive of property by law exempt from execution; that I have property in the State of ——, liable to execution, of the value of more than five hundred dollars.

——————————————————

Subscribed in my presence by ————, and by him sworn to before me this —— day of ——, A. D. 187 .

——————————————————

The above form of bond is applicable, also, to removals under section 633, sub-division 1, of the Revised Statutes, formerly section 12 of the Judiciary Act. If the removal is under sub-division 2 of said section 639, by the non-resident

defendant, the *condition* of the bond may be modified, as
prescribed by this section, to enter and file in, etc., on,
etc., " copies of all process, pleadings, depositions, testimony, and all other proceedings in the cause concerning or
affecting the petitioner for the removal in a certain suit or
action now pending," etc., as in the preceding form.

PETITION FOR REMOVAL by the NON-RESIDENT DEFENDANT UNDER THE REVISED STATUTES, SEC. 639, SUBDIVISION 2, FORMERLY THE ACT OF JULY 27, 1866.

Describe the parties, the State court in which the suit is
pending, as in the preceding petition, stating particularly
the citizenship of each of the plaintiffs and each of the defendants—the amount or value in dispute, as in the preceding form. Then insert in the petition for removal a statement that the said suit in the said State court is one in
which there can be a final determination of the controversy,
so far as concerns the petitioner, without the presence of
the other defendants as parties in the cause. [No affidavit
of prejudice or local influence is required.] Then offer
surety as in preceding petition, and pray removal of the
cause, so far as concerns the petitioner for the removal, as
in the foregoing form.

Form of PETITION *for Removal on the ground of* CITIZEN-
SHIP, *under the Act of March 3, 1875, where the Adversary Parties are all Citizens of different States, and all
the Plaintiffs or all the Defendants unite in the Petition
for Removal.*

IN THE ——— COURT OF ——— COUNTY, STATE OF ———— .

Plaintiff.	Petition for removal to the Circuit
vs.	Court of the United States, District of
Defendant.	——— .

To Said ——— Court :

Your Petitioner respectfully shows to this Honorable Court that the matter and amount in dispute in the above entitled suit exceeds, exclusive of costs, the sum or value of five hundred dollars.

That the controversy in said suit is between citizens of different States, and that the Petitioner was, at the time of the commencement of this suit, and still is, a citizen of the State of ——, and that ———— was then, and still is, a citizen of the State of ——, and that ——— was then, and still is, a citizen of the State of ——. [Here give in like manner the citizenship of each of the several plaintiffs and defendants in the cause.]*

And your petitioner offers herewith a bond with good and sufficient surety for his entering in said Circuit Court of the United States, on the first day of its next session, a copy of the record in this suit, and for paying all costs that may be awarded by said Circuit Court, if said Court shall hold that this suit was wrongfully or improperly removed thereto.

And he prays this Honorable Court to proceed no further herein, except to make the order of removal required by law, and to accept the said surety and bond, and to cause the record herein to be removed into said Circuit Court of the United States in and for the District of ——, and he will ever pray.

Attorneys for Petitioner.

The act of 1875 does not require the petition for the removal to be verified; but, as affording an assurance that the application is made in good faith, a verification may very properly be added, which may be in the following form:

STATE OF ——. }
—— County. } ss.

I. ————, being duly sworn, do say that I am a member of the firm of ————, the attorneys for the petitioner in the above entitled cause; that I have read the foregoing petition, and know the contents thereof; and that the statements and allegations therein contained are true, as I verily believe.

Subscribed by the said ———— in my presence, and by him sworn to before me, this the —— day of ——, A. D. 187 .

If, however, all the parties plaintiff or defendant do not join in the application for the removal, and the application is made under the latter clause of sec. 2 of the act of March 3, 1875, by part of the plaintiffs or part of the defendants actually interested in the controversy, follow the preceding form down to the star (*), giving the citizenship of each of the plaintiffs and defendants, and then add the following :

> Your Petitioner states that. in the said suit above mentioned, there is a controversy which is wholly between citizens of different States. and which can be fully determined as between them. to wit. a controversy between the said petitioner and the said ————. the said ———— and the said ————, [naming the parties actually interested in the said controversy].

If the nature of the controversy does not fully appear in the pleadings, it may be advisable to add a statement of the facts showing the case to be one within the latter clause of sec. 2 of the act of March 3, 1875. After which let the petition follow the form above given.

If the PETITION FOR REMOVAL is on the ground that the suit is one " *arising under the Constitution or Laws of the United States, or treaties made under their authority,*" it is not necessary to state the citizenship of the parties. It is, however, proper to do so ; and if there are several parties, and the transaction in controversy is complex, it may be advisable to state the citizenship of each. The preceding form can, therefore, be followed down to the star (*), and then there may be added the following :

> Your Petitioner states that the said suit is one arising under the laws of the United States. in this, to wit : [Here state the facts which show the Federal character of the case; see *ante*. secs. 2 and 8.]

After which let the petition continue as in the form above given.

Form of BOND *for the removal of a cause under the act of March 3, 1875.*

KNOW ALL MEN BY THESE PRESENTS :

> That I. ————, as principal. and ————. as sureties. are held and firmly bound unto —— in the penal sum of —— dollars, the payment whereof well and truly to be made unto the said ————, heirs and assigns. we bind ourselves. our heirs. representatives and assigns, jointly and severally, firmly by these presents.
>
> Yet. upon these conditions : The said ———— having petitioned the

—— Court of —— County. State of ——. for the removal of a certain
cause therein pending, wherein ———— plaintiff, and ———— defendant , to the Circuit court of the United States in and for the District of ——.

Now, if the said ————. your petitioner, shall enter in the said
Circuit court of the United States, on the first day of its next session, a
copy of the record in said suit, and shall well and truly pay all costs
that may be awarded by said Circuit court of the United States, if said
court shall hold that said suit was wrongfully or improperly removed
thereto [*if special bail was originally requisite in said cause, then add* "and
shall then and there appear and enter special bail in said suit "] then
this obligation to be void; otherwise, in full force and virtue.

Witness our hands and seals, this —— day of ——. A. D. 187 .

——————— —— [L. S.]

——— ——— [L. S.]

——— [L. S.]

It is advisable that the sureties justify, but it is not absolutely necessary. Form of justification, see *supra*, at the
end of the form of bond under the act of March 2, 1867.

Form of Writ of CERTIORARI *under Sec. 7 of the Act of*
March 3, 1875.

THE PRESIDENT OF THE UNITED STATES OF AMERICA TO THE JUDGE
OF THE COURT OF [here describe the State court by name].

Whereas it hath been represented to the Circuit court of the United
States for the District of ——. that a certain suit was commenced in the
—— court of [here name the State court] wherein ————. a citizen
of the State of ——. was plaintiff and ————. a citizen of the State
of ——. was defendant, and that the said ———— duly filed in the said
State court his petition for the removal of said cause into the said Circuit court of the United States. and filed with said petition the bond
with surety required by the act of Congress of March 3. 1875, entitled
" an act to determine the jurisdiction of the Circuit courts of the United
States. and to regulate the removal of causes from State courts and for
other purposes." and that the clerk of the said State court above-named
has refused to the said petitioner for the removal of said cause a copy of
the record therein. though his legal fees therefor were tendered by the
said petitioner :

YOU. THEREFORE. ARE HEREBY COMMANDED that you forthwith certify, or cause to be certified, to the said Circuit court of the United States for the District of ——, a full, true and complete copy of the record and proceedings in the said cause, in which the said petition for removal was filed as aforesaid, plainly and distinctly, and in as full and ample a manner as the same now remain before you, together with this writ; so that the said Circuit court may be able to proceed thereon and do what shall appear to them of right ought to be done. Herein fail not.

[SEAL.]   Witness the Honorable Morrison R. Waite, Chief-Justice of the Supreme Court, and the seal of the said Circuit court hereto affixed this the —— day of ——, A. D. 187 .

Clerk of said Circuit Court.

The writ of certiorari should be directed to the judge or judges of the State court, but a return to the writ duly certified may be made, it is supposed, by the clerk of the said court. Stewart v. Engle, 9 Wheat. 426. See Bacon's Abridg., title *Certiorari; ante*, sec. 10.

INDEX.

A.

ABATEMENT.

Plea in, proper practice where the petition sets out, as ground of removal, facts that are not true, 75.

Motion to remand and plea in abatement contrasted: grounds on which each proceeds, 75.

ADMINISTRATORS. See Executors and Administrators.

AFFIDAVIT.

Of *prejudice or local influence*, under the act of 1867, by whom made, 61, 62.

Need not state reasons or facts showing the local influence, etc, 62.

May be *taken* and *certified* in conformity with the local laws, 62. n. 94.

Infants and persons *non compos mentis*, need not, and can not, make affidavit, 62.

Reasons why affidavit should not always be required to be made by the party himself, 62.

The proper practice, where attorney or agent makes it. 62.

ALIENS.

Right of, to remove suit against *civil officers*, etc., under sec. 644 of Rev. Stats., 6. 7.

Can not remove suit, under Judiciary Act (Rev. Stats., § 640, subdivision 1), 19, n. 25.

Alienage as the ground of Federal jurisdiction. 19, n. 25.

Resident unnaturalized foreigners, deemed aliens, 19, n. 25. See also, 48, n. 65.

Indians, not aliens, 19, n. 25.

Alienage, no cause of removal under act of 1867. 23, n. 32.

A *state* can not make the subject of a foreign government a citizen of the United States, 48, n. 65.

Corporations chartered by foreign countries, deemed aliens for purposes of removal, 51.

AMENDMENTS.

In the pleadings, allowed after removal, 43.

CONSTITUTIONAL LAW.—*Continued.*

And injunction will be granted to restrain revocation of license under such statute. 13, n. 16.

Constitutionality of the act of 1866, 20, n. 26.

And that of the act of 1867 adjudged by the Supreme Court. 25.

Whether Congress has repealed it. 25.

Constitutional limitations of the Federal judicial power, 30 *et seq.*

CONTINUANCE.

Effect of continuance, *by consent,* of cause that was at issue and could have been tried, under act of 1875, 58.

CORPORATIONS. See also JOINT STOCK COMPANIES.

Suit against *Federal,* when removable under act of July 27, 1868 (Rev. Stats., sec. 640), 7, n. 6.

Scope of the act;—what corporations excluded from its operation; conditions essential to make it operative. 7–9.

Officers of, as defendants to a bill in equity, when, and in what sense, *nominal* parties. 17.

Corporations are citizens of state, that created them. 49.

Citizenship of members immaterial, and averment or proof thereof incompetent. 49.

Municipal corporations governed by same principle for jurisdictional purposes. 49, 50.

Citizenship of corporation chartered by different states: its effect on jurisdiction. 49, n. 67.

Effect of different companies constructing same line of road, 49, n. 67.

Effect of consolidation of different companies. 49, n. 67.

Citizenship of consolidated company. 49, n. 67.

Right of foreign corporation to remove cause, not affected by state legislation authorizing *service of process on its agent* in the state. 51.

And its citizenship not affected even by its own assent to be sued in another state. 51.

Corporations within the contemplation of the removal acts, though they can make affidavit only through their proper officers. 61.

President and general manager of railway company, *prima facie* authorized to make the affidavit. 61, 62.

Case where the *solicitor* of the corporation defendant was held authorized to verify petition. 62.

Superintendent of railway company, when only competent to make affidavit. 62.

COSTS.

In suits removed from State courts, by what statutes governed, 42.

D.

DECLARATION. See PRACTICE AND PLEADING.

INDEX. 93

DEFENSE.

What is a defense "arising under the Constitution," etc., "of the United States?" Act of July 27. 1868, discussed; its scope and operation. 7–9.

DISMISSAL. See REMANDING CAUSE.

DOMICILE.

The only essential element of state citizenship, for jurisdictional purposes. 48. n. 65.

Effect of *bona fide* change of. on citizenship. 48. n. 65.

E.

EJECTMENT.

Ejectment suit not removable under acts of March 3. 1863. and March 2, 1867. 7. n. 4.

But otherwise, under act of 1875, 37, n. 49.

EMINENT DOMAIN.

Suit to determine value of private property which an incorporated company seeks to appropriate under the right of. removable. 36, n. 47; 38, n. 49.

ENTERING AN APPEARANCE.

Meaning of. construed and applied. 18. 19 n. 24.

State court allowing an appearance to be entered *nunc pro tunc.* does not restore right of removal under sec. 12 of Judiciary Act. 52. n. 77.

EQUITY.

Bill in. to reform an insurance policy, is such an *original* suit as may be removed. 36, n. 47; 38. n. 49.

Parties to bill in. filed in behalf of complainant and *such others as might come in.* etc., 49, n. 65.

Chancery cause. when only triable. 58.

Application for its removal, when in time, under act of 1875, 58.

Whether laches in making up issues will defeat right of removal. 58.

Effect of local law or practice requiring replication to complete the issue. in absence of laches on part of party applying for removal, 58.

ESTATES.

Removability of suits for the establishment of claims against the estates of deceased persons. 38, 39.

ESTOPPEL.

Acts of party entitled to removal, that will estop him to apply for it, 73. 74. n. 122.

EXECUTORS AND ADMINISTRATORS.

Citizenship of. how affects Federal jurisdiction. 48. n. 66.

Such citizenship disregarded in what actions. 48. n. 66.

Citizenship of executors, how determined. 48. n. 66.

Effect of removal of executor to another state. 48. n. 66.

7

P.

PARTIES.

    Who are, and who are not, *nominal* parties, 17, n. 22.

    Nominal parties, as affecting the right of removal, 17, n. 22.

    Fraudulent joinder of parties. 17. n. 22.

    Officers of a corporation, in what sense *nominal* parties as defendants to a bill in equity, 17, n. 22.

    In an action for *joint indebtedness*, under the acts of 1866 and 1867, 18, n. 23.

    Parties entitled to removal under Judiciary Act, 14, 15. See also 47.

    Parties entitled to removal under act of 1866. 20, 21. See also, 47, 57.

    · Parties entitled to removal under act of 1867, 23, 24. See also, 48.

    Joinder of resident and non-resident plaintiffs under this act, 24.

    Necessary party, though refused by State court the right to become a party, entitled to removal, 35.

    Parties entitled to removal under act of March 3, 1875, Sec. XII, pp. 47–52.

    Citizenship of the *parties to the record* alone determines the jurisdiction,—not that of parties beneficially interested, 48.

    Who are parties to a bill in equity filed by complainant in behalf of himself and *such others as might come in*, etc.. 49, n. 66.

PARTNERS.

    Right of one of several copartners to remove cause as to himself under act of 1866, 57.

PETITION.

    Verification of, under sec. 12 of Judiciary Act, 18, n. 24.

    Requisites of, under Rev. Stats., § 639, 61.

    Under act of 1867 (Rev. Stats.. § 639, sub-div. 3), 61.

    Requisites, function and effect of petition, under act of March 3, 1875, 63, 64.

    No necessity of verification. 63,

    When necessary to state that the case is one " arising under the Constitution, or laws or treaties of the United States," 64.

    Effect of petition and bond for removal on jurisdiction of State court, Sec. XV, pp. 66–70.

    A petition founded on the act of 1867, though showing no right under that act, held sufficient to effect removal under act of 1866, 67, n. 107.

    The filing of petition and bond with the clerk of the State court in vacation, *ipso facto* ousts the jurisdiction of State court, 70.

    Amendment of, after removal had. when allowed, 71.

    The facts set out in. subject of inquiry by the Federal courts exclusively, 75.

    Forms of petitions for removal. See Appendix.

PLEADING. See Practice and Pleading.

100 INDEX.

S.

SETTLEMENT OF ESTATES. See Estates.

SLANDER.

An action of, when removable under "Force Act." 6, n. 4.

SPLITTING ACTION.

Under the act of 1866. Obvious purpose; probable reason for, 21.

Not admissible under act of 1867. 23, n. 32.

Nor under the act of 1875, 29.

STATE COURTS.

From what courts removal may be had. Sec. X. pp. 43 and 44.

Proceedings in. after removal, not stayed by writ from Federal court. 45. note.

Do not embrace "Justices of the Peace." within the meaning of the act of 1867. 53.

Nor *Territorial* courts. within the meaning of the act of 1875, even after admission of the territory as a state, where the suit was brought in the territorial court. 59.

Duty of. upon filing of proper petition and offer of sufficient surety, 66 *et seq.*

Whether *order* of removal is necessary. where the petition presents a case within the removal acts. 67. 68.

Exercise of jurisdiction by State court. subsequent to filing of petition and bond. erroneous. 67.

Jurisdiction not ousted. where petition and pleadings do not show removable case, 69.

Semble. same principle applies. where no security or bond was offered. 69.

Quære, whether State court has power. under act of 1875, to judge of the sufficiency of surety offered. 69.

An erroneous determination. by the State court. of the sufficiency or insufficiency of a petition, neither confers nor ousts Federal jurisdiction, 70.

SUBJECT-MATTER.

In respect of, what suits may be removed under act of 1875. 27.

The subject-matter of the controversy must be money. or something capable of pecuniary estimation. 45.

Requisites of petition in regard to. under act of 1875. 63.

SUITS.

Nature of, that may be removed. under special statutes, 6, 7, 9.

Under the Judiciary Act. 15 *et seq.*

Under the act of 1866, 20.

Under the act of 1867, 23 *et seq.*

Under the act of 1875. 26 *et seq.*, 33.

Suits involving construction of the *bankrupt act*, removable under act of 1875. 33.

www.ingramcontent.com/pod-product-compliance
Lightning Source LLC
Chambersburg PA
CBHW030629270326
41927CB00007B/1357